D0213840

TEACHING IN HIGHER EDUCATION

SUCCESS IN RESEARCH

The Success in Research series has been designed by Cindy Becker and Pam Denicolo to provide short, authoritative and accessible guides for students, researchers and academics on the key area of professional and research development.

Each book is written with an eye to avoiding jargon and each aims to cut to the chase of what readers really need to know about a given topic. These are practical and supportive books and will be essential reading for any students or researchers interested in developing their skills and broadening their professional and methodological knowledge in an academic context.

SUCCESS IN RESEARCH

TEACHING IN HIGHER EDUCATION

LUCINDA BECKER ⚲ PAM DENICOLO

Los Angeles | London | New Delhi
Singapore | Washington DC

Los Angeles | London | New Delhi
Singapore | Washington DC

SAGE Publications Ltd
1 Oliver's Yard
55 City Road
London EC1Y 1SP

SAGE Publications Inc.
2455 Teller Road
Thousand Oaks, California 91320

SAGE Publications India Pvt Ltd
B 1/I 1 Mohan Cooperative Industrial Area
Mathura Road
New Delhi 110 044

SAGE Publications Asia-Pacific Pte Ltd
3 Church Street
#10-04 Samsung Hub
Singapore 049483

Editor: Katie Metzler
Assistant editor: Anna Horvai
Production editor: Ian Antcliff
Copyeditor: Michelle Clark
Proofreader: Louise Harnby
Marketing manager: Catherine Slinn
Cover design: Lisa Harper
Typeset by: C&M Digitals (P) Ltd, Chennai, India
Printed and bound by: CPI Group (UK) Ltd,
Croydon, CR0 4YY

MIX
Paper from
responsible sources
FSC   FSC® C013604
www.fsc.org

© Lucinda Becker and Pam Denicolo 2013

First published 2013

Apart from any fair dealing for the purposes of research
or private study, or criticism or review, as permitted under
the Copyright, Designs and Patents Act, 1988, this
publication may be reproduced, stored or transmitted in
any form, or by any means, only with the prior permission
in writing of the publishers, or in the case of reprographic
reproduction, in accordance with the terms of licences
issued by the Copyright Licensing Agency. Enquiries
concerning reproduction outside those terms should be
sent to the publishers.

Library of Congress Control Number: 2012947043

British Library Cataloguing in Publication data

A catalogue record for this book is available from
the British Library

ISBN 978–1-4462–5604-6
ISBN 978–1-4462–5605-3 (pbk)

CONTENTS

ABOUT THE AUTHORS

Dr Lucinda Becker, an award winning Senior Lecturer in the Department of English Literature at the University of Reading, and University Teaching Fellow, has spent her career committed to enhancing the skills and knowledge of undergraduates and research postgraduates. She has written numerous successful study skills guides for students. As a professional trainer she also works throughout the United Kingdom and Europe, devising and delivering training in communication and management techniques, principally to lawyers, engineers and scientists.

Professor Pam Denicolo, a chartered constructivist psychologist, found her early research commitment to generally improving learning and teaching in Higher Education focusing progressively on the needs of graduate students, their supervisors and other professionals seeking to develop their practice. This passion is demonstrated through her numerous successful doctoral candidates and her leading roles in national and international organisations such as the UK Council for Graduate Education, the International Study Association on Teachers and Teaching, the Society for Research into Higher Education Postgraduate Network, the Impact and Evaluation Group and other working groups of Vitae, and the QAA Doctoral Characteristics Advisory Group, all of which have resulted in many publications, presentations and workshops. She maintains these contacts and has developed others after becoming Emeritus at Reading, including enjoying a new role as advocate for Graduate Studies at the University of Surrey.

Cindy and Pam worked exuberantly together for many years, managing and developing the Graduate School at the University of Reading and providing a substantial contribution to its Research Methods, Generic Skills and Doctoral Supervisor training. They continue to enjoy writing together.

One

INTRODUCTION

If any of us were to pause for a moment to think about teaching in universities and similar institutions we might be struck by a paradox. Generally speaking, our formative education is spent with each of us saying 'look how much I know' or 'see, this is how clever I am'. We are praised for this, encouraged to focus principally on our needs as learners and then researchers, and we expect to be rewarded for our talents and efforts. What is the reward? Well, some more research time (we expect), some sense of security, both practical and intellectual (we hope) and … teaching. This last is, of course, entirely illogical. Why should we be good educators, or even want to be good teachers, just because we are intellectually impressive and research motivated? Where is the incentive and, just as importantly, where is the skill?

In the past this conundrum was either overlooked entirely or dismissed as a minor foible of our education system. It assumed that if you were expert in your field you would be able, by some ill-defined means, to teach others. In some situations (and many of us will no doubt remember these), the onus was clearly on the learner to learn rather than on the erudite, brilliant researcher to teach. Pearls of wisdom would drop casually from the lips of a master into the eager hands of followers. This presumably worked well for Socrates – it is not going to work for anyone today.

It is said that J. R. R. Tolkien gave all of his lectures at Oxford with his back to the auditorium. In today's world, he would struggle with this approach. By the time he had mastered the nuances of formative v. summative assessment, coursework v. exam-led modules, extra-curricula v. intra-curricula placement learning and student-led seminar groups he would probably be delighted to have had the chance to turn around and remind himself of the point of teaching: the students.

The individuality of the educator should be defended within higher education as one of the hallmarks of our much-admired system; as long as an approach stimulates learning, then we would encourage it. The aim of this book, therefore, is not to foster a 'one approach fits all' attitude towards teaching, but, rather, to allow you to explore this area of your life as a researcher.

Having made that point, it would be unfair not to warn you of a significant difference between the approach others will take towards you as a researcher and that which you might experience as a lecturer. As a researcher, much is done to foster your well-being, encourage your intellectual development and support you as you produce excellent, groundbreaking research. As an educator, you are required to fit into a system, within what is currently a relatively tough educational environment. Although the work can be hugely rewarding, much less attention will be paid to your individual needs: the task is all and the system can feel overwhelming at times.

Throughout this book we will be urging you to talk to your supervisor or mentor about how to make your situation most conducive to your development as an educator and researcher, but you need to be aware that it may not be possible for changes to be made to accommodate your needs. You are probably already used to this in many areas of your life and this experience will help you now.

We cannot know exactly which stage of the life of a teacher would apply to you as you read this book for the first time. You might be a postgraduate research student, an early career researcher or a far more experienced academic faced with a new challenge. You might expect to be teaching only what pertains directly to your specialism or you might (as is far more likely) be expected to teach more broadly. You might be teaching students at any stage of their career or you might be using your teaching skills to disseminate your research and knowledge to a much wider field. Whatever your situation, we can help.

Although we can know relatively little about you, we do know that you are taking your task as an educator seriously, so you do not want to waste your valuable research time inventing 'new' teaching methods when the work has already been done for you, and that you are open to advice. You can also learn here something about us, right here at the outset.

Cindy's life in teaching began in the world of professional training and the idea of teaching in academia was far from her mind for many years. As a trainer in a variety of communication and management skills, she was used to holding the attention of adults for two-day courses. Working principally with scientists, lawyers and engineers, she developed an appreciation of the work of different fields and came to enjoy the range of ways in which people approached similar problems. Alongside her training life, she dabbled in other areas – teaching A-level students, being an agony aunt for a local newspaper, acting as a website study adviser and counselling people through career change management.

Even as Cindy began her doctoral research, her focus gravitated to research rather than teaching. As a mature postgraduate student, grappling with English literature and social history, she came to understand much about how she learned; her research also created enthusiasm to share both her knowledge and her intellectual curiosity with others. For her, a love of teaching students hit her the moment she took her first seminar group. It was not even a very good seminar, despite all of her overpreparation, but she knew she could get better and the better she got, the more likely she was to see that spark of recognition and understanding in her students' eyes.

Pam began teaching in a technical college – a baptism of fire since, as a science teacher, she was expected not only to teach A level subjects but also aid hairdressers' understanding of the chemical processes of perms and dyes and the lifecycle of head lice. She wanted to inspire her students and so undertook a teaching qualification part-time concurrently with some Open University courses that eventually culminated in a first class honours degree in psychology, particularly related to learning. This experience came in handy when she was pursuing her doctorate because she was able to undertake teaching duties on a course designed for all those whose job encompassed in some way the teaching of adults, which soon led to an academic post that involved designing courses for academics to learn how to teach more effectively.

The focus of Pam's doctorate and her subsequent research and academic teaching became the same – finding ways to improve student learning, particularly in higher education – and led to an exciting life, wandering the universities of the world as a provider of workshops on student learning and academic teaching for the British Council, in addition to her normal but related research, writing and teaching duties in the UK. Over time, her interest became further focused on developing the support and training of research students and led to her establishing a graduate school with a large range of courses and other forms of support for postgraduate students. It was at this point that she met up with and began her joyful collusion with an intellectual soulmate, Cindy.

Together, we set out to enliven and enrich the intellectual lives of postgraduate researchers at our university. An ambitious goal, we know, but one that we believed we could achieve. We designed courses to suit the changing needs of researchers in a competitive and fast-moving world; as much as possible we tried to anticipate their cultural and emotional needs as well as their academic requirements; we worked with our peers to offer the best possible support and training, drawing on the skills of colleagues from all over our university; most of all, we had fun. What has been confirmed for us during our time together is that learning to teach is fundamental: sharing your ideas and helping others to find their intellectual path is the richest reward. Beyond that there is a world of challenges, of course, but we are both still at our happiest when we are standing in front of (or sitting beside) a group of learners, making things happen.

We do not believe that any one method works for all teachers or for all students in all situations. What we do believe is that there are many approaches that can work and some of them will suit you and the ways in which your students tend to respond. It is for this reason that the guide is crammed full of ideas and guidance points.

This is also why we make just one request of our readers: be open to ideas. Be prepared to try an approach and, if it is not exactly what you want, be bold about adapting or even abandoning it. If you can be sensitive to the responses of your learners you will instinctively know when a method needs some flexing. We say here 'can' be sensitive because this is not necessarily about your willingness to be open to your learners; it simply takes a fair bit of confidence to allow yourself to do this. We would fully expect that for your first lecture, for example, your experience would be similar to ours – you find yourself in a surreal world of terror in which you can do little more than follow your script and hope that you make it through to the end without making a fool of yourself (for the details of how this did not work for one of the authors, see Chapter 6!). As your confidence grows, so will your ability to judge the feel of a lecture theatre and gauge how much your audience would appreciate digressions, for example. At that point, a lecture can be a pleasure to give. This guide will show you that there are many ways to succeed and it will help you to get there more quickly and surefootedly than you would on your own.

Ways to use this book

We anticipate that you will use this book in several ways. You could read it through in its entirety, especially if teaching is a new venture for you. You might, perhaps, just look at certain chapters as the need arises. If you want a quick boost as you face new situations, you could then revisit a chapter to check out the main points. Over time, you will need the detailed guidance less often, but may find it interesting to return to some of the theoretical points. If you are ever lacking in ideas, the handy top tips will be there for you. If you are ever lacking in inspiration, the boxes on how research and teaching dovetail will be there, too. If you are ever lacking courage, the 'voice of experience' feature will remind you that others have been there before you and you are not alone.

The exercises in the guide serve two purposes. They will help you to develop your thoughts and skills in an area, but they will also act as a record of how you feel about teaching and how you foresee your progress. This type of reflection is valuable in itself, of course, but we also hope that it will be of benefit to you in the future. As you face new teaching challenges, you will be able to remind yourself of how this felt before and, when you are in a position to mentor others in their teaching, you will recall the learning process that you went through.

It is because we know that the guide could be used in many ways that we have constructed it as we have. The main text of each chapter offers practical advice on teaching and, within this advice, you will also find, as mentioned, step-by-step exercises, top tips, checklists and examples, as well as boxes that give you the opportunity to think more broadly about the task you are facing, allowing you to ponder both how a teaching situation might feed into your research and the theories of teaching underpinning the advice we are offering. As we have experience of teaching triumphs *and* disasters, we sometimes offer a 'word of warning' box.

Terminology may occasionally crop up as an issue as we go through the guidance with you, so we will define terms whenever we feel there could be any confusion. This is not to suggest in any way that you do not know basic teaching terminology. Rather, we define terms because we know that institutions use them differently and we want you to know exactly what we mean for the purposes of this book. A tutorial, for example, can mean a one-to-one learning session with a student or a session with one or more students to discuss their essays or other coursework, or a more general group learning session. Our aim is to ensure the smoothest possible transition of knowledge from us to you, whatever your circumstances or experience.

Two
WHY TEACH?

Your initial answer to this may be 'I have no real idea' or 'because someone asked me to do it' and these would not be uncommon responses, because many of us have never thought to ask ourselves, or others, this question. If pressed, you might move on to some pragmatic reasons: 'I need the money' or 'I had better get some practice in, ready for the future'.

Too often, teaching is seen as a 'fallback' position, so this instinctive reaction is not all that surprising when one considers the life of established academics. They teach, but also bid for research funding so as to gain leave to do their research. So, in effect, it could appear as if the majority of academics are teaching while doing their best to escape from teaching, which leads sometimes to the assumption that teaching is 'getting in the way'. Of course, for the vast majority of academics, teaching is a joyful experience, inspiring and exciting, but you need to think about it so that you can clearly distinguish what you hope to achieve by teaching and how you and your students will benefit from your efforts.

If teaching and research are structurally in opposition to each other, and our higher education system lends itself to the creation of this tension, it is too easy to see teaching as a chore, a negative activity that deprives you of time to carry out research. We all hear about institutions as research-intensive and successful in gaining research funding, but we must also be aware of the need to appeal to students who are paying increasingly large fees and expect an excellent learning experience. This necessarily makes teaching not just a core function of higher education but also one at which it makes sense to excel in terms of your career progression.

So, already we can see that the initial responses we suggested above need to be nuanced to include, at the very least, 'because I need to succeed in this area'. We would also hope that you could add some far more positive responses to the list. For those of us who love teaching, it becomes an end in and of itself, an activity that defines much of our intellectual life. We would not expect you just yet to be able to reel off a huge list of reasons, positive or not, as to why you are teaching or about to teach, but now would be a good time to pause and give it some thought. The exercise below might help you to focus on your motivation. Take stock of your situation and consider for a minute: why are you doing this?

 EXERCISE 1

List below four of your reasons for teaching:

1

2

3

4

The next exercise seems more negative, but, if you can define some of your anxieties at this early stage, it will help you to be more targeted in your approach as you use this book.

 EXERCISE 2

Now list four things about teaching that worry you the most:

1

2

3

4

Although there is much value to be gained from such reflection, it is also beneficial to hear about the experiences of others. So, in writing this guide, we asked experienced academics (who have been teaching for between 5 and 35 years) about their lives as educators and we share their comments with you throughout the book. The following is the first of these.

THE VOICE OF EXPERIENCE

What worried you most about teaching when you first started out? The academics' responses to this question were repeated in one form or another across the range of disciplines. Here is what they said.

'I worried that I would forget everything I knew, so I wrote down everything I could think of in preparation for the lecture.'

'What if they just don't listen – just ignore me – what would I do?'

'It took much experience before the constant niggle subsided that I would look such a fool if they asked me something and I didn't know the answer.'

'There just seemed to be so much to tell them about my subject that I didn't know where to begin and what could conceivably be missed out in the first session.'

You may already have noticed the constant stress in higher education on 'teaching and learning' rather than just teaching. This is a useful reminder to us all that there is an outcome of what we do. Although the focus of this book is, naturally, on you and how you will cope with different situations as you become a successful educator, you will be helped in this hugely by reminding yourself at frequent intervals that the experience of the learner is the test by which you will be gauging all of your successes. Our thoughts now, therefore, turn to your students in the next exercise.

 EXERCISE 3

What personal qualities do you possess that could make you a successful teacher?

1

2

3

4

5

You will probably find this a difficult exercise to do. We all tend to be too modest and, at this stage, you might struggle to identify the qualities that will make you a good teacher. This might be an exercise to which you will return in future, as your experience and confidence grows.

The next exercise might be equally challenging. This is not because you do not anticipate being a very 'giving' educator, but more because we are not usually required to define exactly what we as individuals offer our students, what makes each of us special. For this reason, it is likely that this, too, will be an exercise to which you return repeatedly as you work through this book.

 EXERCISE 4

What do you want your teaching to give to your students?

1

2

3

4

5

Again, we thought you might like to hear about the experiences of others, to help shape your approach to the task ahead.

THE VOICE OF EXPERIENCE

What do you feel that you give to your students? These are some of the responses given by our group of experienced academics. Again, they were similar across disciplines.
'A sense of excitement and wonderment about the topic.'
'The stimulus to want to find out more for themselves.'
'Confidence that they *could* understand, with a bit of effort, the complexities of [discipline area].'
'A challenge to their current ways of thinking … opening up new horizons, perhaps.'

Having considered with you some of the many reasons for wanting to teach and for you becoming a successful teacher, we want here to return to the conundrum we outlined at the beginning of this chapter: the potential tension between teaching and research. This tension can be intellectual ('I am so immersed in my research that I do not want to change tack and teach today'), practical ('Do I really have time to teach this week?') and emotional ('There is so much pressure on me at the moment'). It can also be a hugely creative tension, once we come to see that these are not two separate activities but two parts of the intellectual whole of our lives. Throughout this guide, we will be reminding you of this by including boxes such as this one.

TEACHING AND YOUR RESEARCH

For us, teaching, learning and research are tightly clustered concepts, each with many aspects in common with the others, at least in terms of process, principles and values. Indeed, it is hardly possible to do one without at least one of the others being involved, too. It is a symbiotic relationship, each gaining from involvement with the other.

Learning is a relatively permanent change in behaviour as a result of experience. It involves the association of ideas, memory, thought, experience, some kind of activity motivated towards some end. Individuals learn best when actively engaged in learning; learning is seen to be more persistent when it seems to be personally relevant and involves an exploration of and challenge to current ideas – a kind of personal research!

The task of the teacher is to find ways of actively engaging people in their learning, exploring ways of making it personally relevant and meaningful to the learner by building on what they already know while challenging current perspectives. Similarly, research depends on building on what is already known while considering alternative perspectives that are tested against experience to generate new hypotheses.

You might like to think of teaching and learning being two parallel strands, each working well when entwined with each other and working even better if linked occasionally by bonds of research ... with a reproductive and developmental function ... a bit like the double helix of DNA!

How much can I handle?

However much you may come to see teaching as a productive and intellectually satisfying experience, you will always need to know your limits – this is especially true in the early days. There might be many different pressures on you to teach (financial, professional, personal), but you are unlikely to do it well if you push yourself too far when you are starting out. This is partly because, when you are less experienced, it can seem as if even a moderate amount of teaching is taking over your life. We can pretty much guarantee that the first lecture you give will dominate your day, if not your week, and the first few seminars will certainly take far longer to prepare than to lead. This is inevitable and need not be a problem, as long as you have planned for it.

 WORD OF WARNING

At the outset, you are likely to need around two to three times as long to prepare a teaching session as you need to deliver it, so factor this into your time planning.

Of course, as your confidence increases and you gain more experience, it is easier to put teaching into its correct place in your working life, giving it the attention it deserves but not allowing the experience to overwhelm you. Until then, some caution is needed. Interestingly, for most scholars this is less about workload and more about their work pattern.

Think now about how you tend to work. Do you prefer a complete day dedicated to one research task or are you more productive when you can vary your tasks? Do you work best in one- or two-hour bursts or do you need far more time to settle your mind into what you are doing? Do you find yourself easily flustered if you are interrupted?

These types of questions will give you an idea as to what the ideal teaching pattern is for you. Some scholars prefer to teach on two, or perhaps just one, day a week and then be free to get back to their research in an extended stretch for the rest of the week; others thrive on a single teaching session four or five days a week.

We would not want to give the impression here that you are likely, at a moment's notice, to be given a huge teaching schedule and simply be told to get on with it. Some departments, institutions and funding bodies might encourage or require some teaching as part of the workload of their researchers, but this will be modest. If you are working as an early career lecturer, you may have a reduced teaching load in your first year as you will be encouraged to spend a significant amount of your time producing early career research bids or undertaking training. If you are working on a sessional basis, either alongside your research project or as a postdoctoral scholar looking for a permanent position, then it is more likely that you will be looking to secure any teaching that is available, perhaps at more than one institution. In this latter situation the danger of teaching overload is present, but the guidance in this book will at least help you to smooth out many of the bumps you might encounter on the way.

Your overall teaching workload will depend on your individual situation, but if you can decide now on a teaching pattern that might suit you, it could be possible for you to achieve it. We say 'could' because, naturally, other factors come into play than simply your preference. Too often, though, the issue is not that a teaching timetable cannot be changed, but that a researcher does not ask in good time. So, try not to be too diffident about this – it may be no problem at all to change your timetable. If you feel reluctant to ask and then have to make changes at the last minute, that is when a problem is created.

Definition: We will be talking about both 'modules' and 'courses' in this guide, but we see these terms as relatively interchangeable. When we are talking about a suite or series of modules/courses, we will refer to this as a 'programme'.

A word about repeat teaching here. You are likely to be given a range of courses on which to teach and this gives you the opportunity to explore and produce plenty of teaching material, but you might want to consider some repeat teaching. That is, teaching two or more groups who are taking the same module. This has huge timesaving benefits (you prepare one seminar and use the material two or three times).

It does have one pitfall, though: if you are teaching one group at 9 a.m. and then another with the same material an hour later, it can feel like a major case of déjà vu, which can be offputting. Again, talk to course convenors or administrators to see whether repeat teaching is possible, if you think it would work well for you. For instance, you might be able to negotiate a gap between repeat sessions to reduce the worry of 'Have I already said that to this class or was it the previous one?' thoughts. As with timetabling, do it early and with the confidence that you are not causing a problem, simply asking what is possible.

 WORD OF WARNING

We are encouraging you here to be confident and ask if you would prefer to do repeat teaching or if you would find an altered teaching load beneficial. However, remain aware that any teaching system is complicated and it may not be possible to make changes. If this is the case, accept it with good grace and move on: it happens to us all from time to time – we cannot always be given the teaching pattern that we would prefer.

TOP TIP

Communication is going to be vital to your success as a teacher in so many ways. Make the first move and introduce yourself to the module/course convenors for whom you will be teaching (this will not necessarily happen automatically) and always get to know administration staff well enough to feel comfortable asking for their help and advice.

How might I start to teach?

There are several common ways in which a researcher might begin to teach on a formal basis. It might be a condition of your research funding, it could be a traditional part of the activities of researchers within your department, or you might perhaps be offered teaching on a sessional basis (that is, being paid per module you teach) quite separate from your research activity. You might be given plenty of notice (as will be the case if teaching forms part of your funded activity) or have very little warning (if you are asked to stand in for a colleague who takes leave).

However it happens, you can expect that, at all stages of your research, teaching might form part of your daily life, but note that we mentioned teaching 'on a formal basis'. What we would like to do with you here is explore the teaching that you may well have done informally, which is very likely to have an impact on your early teaching experiences in a more formal setting.

The checklist below will give you some examples of situations in which you could already effectively have been teaching, but you may not have chosen to define it as such. Tick off those situations in which you have had some experience and add any other examples you can to the list.

 CHECKLIST

1 Workplace talks (sometimes called 'toolbox talks')
2 Sports coaching
3 One-to-one tuition (a musical instrument, a language, a skill)
4 Leading a team
5 Mentoring
6 Giving a careers talk
7 Helping in a school
8 Being a guest speaker.

9   Helping family or friends with their study.
10 Presenting at or chairing a meeting.
11 Leading an undergraduate seminar as a student.
12 Presenting to a seminar.
13 Teaching someone to cook.
14 Giving a conference paper.
15 Producing written instructions.
16 Giving a theatrical performance.
17 Taking part in a postgraduate research seminar.
18 Explaining how to use any technology.
19 Undertaking a viva.
20 Presenting to a research panel.
21 Giving a presentation at a job interview.
22 Showing someone how to assemble flat-pack furniture.

Now that you know what we mean, you could add your own examples here:

....

....

....

....

....

There are two good reasons for completing this checklist. The first is to demonstrate that you are unlikely to be an entire novice in teaching, even if you
have never taught in a formal teaching situation before. The second is to
dispel for you the myth that teaching can be taught. It is all about utilising
and adapting your experiences. We remember the time when we started
out as teachers, both firmly believing that there must a secret to the art and
that if someone would just tell us the secret, we would transform into successful, perhaps even outstanding, teachers. It can take a long time to realise
that, actually, you always have been a teacher, somewhere inside yourself,
which we all are. We can offer you lots of advice and guidance, and this
helps hugely, but you will turn around in a few years' time and discover that
you have not had to change your personality in order to become an effective academic. You will try out and abandon those suggestions that do not
work for you; you will try out and adapt those which do work.

   If learning to teach is actually about discovering the type of teacher you
naturally are and then playing to your strengths, this process can start for you
here. If you have the time to spare now, look back at the instances above that
you were able to tick and think about how you approached each task.

We are not asking that you spend a huge amount of time listing all of the things that went well, or not so well (although some of that will happen later in this guide), but, rather, we would like you to begin to see yourself, through recalling those experiences, as in part a teacher already, with strengths to rely on as you move forward.

Research seminars

We have mentioned these in the chart above and we want to turn to them again now. We want to focus again for a moment on the strong relationship between research, its processes and dissemination and your role as a teacher.

TEACHING AND YOUR RESEARCH

One fundamental skill required of all researchers is to be able to communicate your ideas to others. As a doctoral student you first need to clarify your ideas to yourself and you will often achieve this by writing them down, crafting them into some shape that others can recognise, or talking your tentative ideas over with colleagues, exploring together what the potential meaning is or could be. In fact, all researchers go through a similar process, having germs of ideas that are often difficult to articulate, struggling to find the right words, then putting them into an order for others to grasp and debate.

Finding the right words means also finding out what words will be meaningful to your audience so you can take them from their current level of understanding to the new one that you are working on. A small group of people whose interests and technical vocabulary is similar to yours is a small step and so a good place to start.

In the next chapter we go into more detail about how to give an effective research seminar to your peers and how this might help you in your teaching more generally.

Three

SEMINAR PRESENTATIONS TO YOUR PEERS

A seminar presentation might not strike you as the most obvious teaching experience, but it is a situation that requires many of the skills you will use in teaching: managing time and resources, articulating your ideas clearly, encouraging and controlling discussion, as well as leaving space for learning. Of course, there are many differences between this circumstance and that of teaching, but it is a good place to start, noticing the similarities and differences and using your past to enhance your future performance.

The title of this chapter is a little wordy, deliberately. Most of what we suggest in this chapter will relate to seminar presentations to your peers at all stages of your academic career, so you might want to bear in mind your time as an undergraduate as well as your more recent experiences. We will be referring throughout to research seminars, but we will assume that you will have undergraduate seminars in your mind also.

Research seminar opportunities

We are conscious as we write this chapter that you might be thinking, 'What do you mean by research seminars?' or even, 'I don't think this section will be relevant to me at all'. What we mean is simple, but you may have used different terminology. We are referring to any situation where you have been explaining your research in a relatively formal situation with a group of your peers. In many cases this would be a regular occurrence as part of a postgraduate research course. It may have been led by an established academic or one of your fellow research students or early career researchers. We are not considering here lunchtime sessions during which you chatted in a group about challenges you all faced, but more the type of situation for which you had to prepare material in advance and deliver that material, usually in the form of a short talk with discussion afterwards or else a lengthier presentation with some questions and answers following.

If none of this is familiar to you or if you recognise the situation but have only attended one or two such occasions and perhaps not spoken up at them, it is not too late to gain some valuable experience in this way. There are several ways in which you could tap into this opportunity.

 CHECKLIST

1   Your department may run research seminars, but they are sometimes advertised to staff via e-mail rather than in the form of notices, so check with your supervisor/mentor.
2   Your department will be part of at least one larger unit (school, faculty), so check for opportunities outsider your department via the institutional website.
3   Don't be afraid to knock on doors: administrative staff will know about when and where a variety of different research seminars are held.
4   Be bold: just because a research seminar theme does not exactly match your narrower field of research, it may still be of value.
5   Check also with your fellow researchers at other universities: going out of your normal milieu to speak about your research can be invigorating even if it is a little daunting.
6   Online research forums may be a way for you to discuss your research and formulate your thoughts, but their value is limited for the purposes of teaching practice.

All of these checklist points assume that you are going to slot into an existing forum for discussion, which would save you time and effort, but it is also worth considering running your own series of research seminars. This would not be an especially onerous task. You would simply need to identify convenient times for perhaps three or four research seminars a term. The administrative staff in your department would be able to arrange a room for you and advertising such a series of events is easy enough via e-mail and online forums.

 TOP TIP

The administrative staff in your department will probably have many years' experience and so will not only be able to help you to arrange research seminars but also be in a position to give you the 'inside information' on what has worked well in the past, advising you on the best times to choose and the most effective way to advertise events. Using their expertise will save you time and hassle.

We are not arguing here that arranging research seminars, or even attending them, is going to be essential at this stage of your career. If you have already attended many of them in the past, it may be a case of simply reflecting on the experience. Equally, if you have a reasonable amount of teaching experience already, you may not need to exploit this opportunity. We would argue, though, that attending and/or organising research seminars is quite an 'easy win' in terms of gaining teaching practice. However, even a relatively easy task needs to be worth your while, so, next, we will consider what you might get out of it.

Why contribute to a research seminar?

We always find research seminars useful: they help us to shape our ideas, offer friendly intellectual support for what we are trying to achieve and remind us of the importance of meeting with like-minded scholars. In earlier times, they helped us to become teachers. Neither of us realised it at the time, but the experience was shaping both our views of ourselves and our understanding of what it means to teach. Offering your research findings in this setting can show you much about the fundamentals of teaching. You will learn to:

1 judge how much material will fill a timespan without overwhelming discussion (it would be rare indeed for anyone to have too little material)
2 present ideas clearly and effectively, using repetition to best effect for complex ideas and material
3 divide your effort between speaking and presenting ideas graphically with the use of handouts, data projector slides, demonstrations and other visual aids to learning
4 manage time in a setting where your peers are happy to stop you if you run over the time they have allocated for the event
5 tailor material to your audience
6 juggle information so that material can be added or excluded without a hitch
7 respect the ideas of others, be able to note them rapidly and respond to them appropriately
8 grasp at speed what someone is trying to say and agree enthusiastically or disagree productively
9 gain confidence without sapping the confidence of others
10 know when to keep quiet so as to allow discussion and learning to happen.

TOP TIP

We will be urging you throughout this book to allow 'space for learning' and this idea perhaps needs some explanation. There is no doubt that when your students are making notes in a lecture they are acquiring information, which is part of the learning process. When they are listening to you in a seminar or tutorial they continue with that learning at a different level and when they are contributing to a seminar discussion they are learning how to articulate their thoughts and use the ideas of others to support their arguments. All of this is vital, but there is another, equally important, moment that only an experienced and sharp-eyed teacher can see. It is the few seconds every now and then when you allow silence to happen. In those moments the students can take a mental breath and digest what is going on, make connections and gather their thoughts ready for the next stage. It takes confidence to let this magic happen, and the ability to see the best moment for it, but if you cram each second with material you will never spot it. Instead, try to feel the rhythm of the learning event, looking out for the place where you could give your students space for learning.

TEACHING AND YOUR RESEARCH

Think about the answers to the following questions.

- What are the key concepts in your research?
- How long did it take for you to get to grips with them?
- What prior information did you have about the area of study when your research started?

The answers to these questions will enable you to gain some appreciation of the task you present to your seminar audience. You will realise that you can probably only deal with one or two of the key concepts in the time available, no matter how well informed your audience is about the background to your research. If they are not well informed about this background then you will need to provide some basic information, so the next question to yourself is: what main things will you need to include to help them bridge from their understandings to those you will present? This is the beginning of the process of selecting your material to suit your audience and the time available.

Preparing the right material

The title of this section seems a little proscriptive, as if there is just one right way to do things. This would be nonsense, of course. You are the best teaching aid you possess and you will make a session work in all sorts of ways, regardless of the material. However, a range of different source materials could contribute to the success of a research seminar. We are not thinking here of the content but, rather, the form in which it is best presented. You have several immediate sources of material in the seminar itself.

1 **An overview** This can be given out as a sheet at the beginning of the seminar or it may be your first data projector slide. It is a good way to keep your peers focused as they can see where you are going and can decide when they might interrupt, if you have given them this option, or begin to think about the questions they want to ask at the end of your talk.
2 **Handouts** For the seminar itself, try to keep the handouts as brief as possible. They need to give essential information, but resist the temptation to use them to explain your points in great detail: that is your job. It is a good idea to leave space on them so that your peers can make their own notes.
3 **Data projector slides** These are used principally to give an overview of a topic area or for inherently visual material, such as pictures, films, graphs, charts and so forth.

 WORD OF WARNING

Data projector slides are sometimes mistakenly thought of as a just another form of handout, but their effect on a group is quite different.

A handout is essentially a private document that can be scrutinised, without comment, repeatedly during an event. It is 'safe' – unlike a data projector slide, it will not disappear. It can also contain far more detail than a slide, because the recipient can check and recheck what is on it, make explanatory notes as you work through the material and note down questions to ask.

A slide needs to be sparse and designed to make a splash, engage and excite an audience or show a point that everyone needs to work through together.

A handout can include more detail, the material can be more complicated than you might put on a slide and it can include references to other sources that the readers might need to refer back to in the future.

You have control over the materials listed above – they are prepared in advance and might be given out during the event or sent to colleagues. There are other categories of materials over which you have far less control, materials that can have great impact but must be handled carefully, if at all.

- **Online material** Essential to some situations, zapping across to the Internet to support your point can be hugely effective. It can also be a disaster, if the connection goes down at the vital moment or the page you need has been updated since you last looked. The odd technical glitch should be no problem, but for the really important information you might consider copying the material on to your data projector slides, if this is practicable.

- **Demonstration** Always nerve-wracking! Also, of course, exciting and engaging for your peers. Just film the demonstration beforehand and store the film ready to show if the demonstration fails to live up to expectations on the day.

- **Interactive smartboard** This piece of equipment can be fairly much under your control if you are using it to view data projector slides with the option to add a point or two to those slides on additional 'notebook' pages (although have a flipchart to hand, just in case). Interactive surveys conducted live through the whiteboard during a seminar are far more of a risk and surprisingly time-consuming, so think carefully before you commit to that means alone to make your point.

- **Film or audiofile** The same benefits and dangers apply here as were mentioned for online materials. Ensure that you have additional materials to fill up any time you suddenly have on your hands because the audiofile or film clip refuses to load.

 TOP TIP

In a research seminar there is no one 'right time' to give out your material, but some conventions do apply. Dense materials that are needed to prepare for the event will be sent out in advance. Copies of slides being shown at the event are given out at the outset if you expect your peers to refer to them repeatedly. If not, decide if giving them out will spoil the element of surprise and excitement you hope to create. A list of references to further reading or very specialised detail can be prepared in advance, but only given to those who ask after the event.

You will see from this that you have a plethora of options for the materials you can produce for a research seminar. We will return to the use of these as teaching aids in later chapters, but there is another factor to take into account now. While the research seminar is your priority when you produce these materials, you will want also to think about recycling materials. Keep copies of every teaching aid you produce. The handouts, slides, films or whatever you produce for a seminar of your peers might, with just a little tweaking, become the perfect support for an undergraduate seminar you are leading or transform into a lecture handout.

WORD OF WARNING

Remember that our focus here is on how to succeed in a research seminar. Although some of the principles will be similar when you are teaching, the details will differ. A lecture will, on the whole, need rather less in the way of materials than a research seminar of the same length because you have more control over the development of the situation. A one-off undergraduate seminar, in contrast, might need a little more than that required for a research seminar if you need to give the students some background and context and some 'take away' points for later consideration.

As you work on materials for a research seminar, use the following to guide you.

CHECKLIST

1   How long will the research seminar last?
2   Is it a 'one off' or one in a series? This will give you a sense of whether or not the group members will be used to meeting together. If they are, they might be more ready to ask probing questions.
3   How formal is the delivery to be? That is, will you be standing giving your talk or sitting? Will you be offering a short series of talking points or a more detailed presentation?
4   How is the time divided up? A short presentation with a lengthy discussion session or a longer presentation with a brief question and answer session?
5   Are you the only speaker or will there be several research presentations during the seminar?
6   How many people are likely to be there? What might be their level of knowledge?
7   Will the group consist of just your fellow researchers or will others be there?
8   Where is it being held? Can you visit the room beforehand? You will want, for example, to make sure that it is big enough but not huge and the seating is arranged in a way which suits what you intend to do.
9   Is there the right technology in the room, if you plan to use it?
10 Are you expected to send some advance reading materials to the group? Would this suit your purpose?

Getting the tone right

Leading an undergraduate seminar, although a little daunting in prospect, can actually be far less nerve-wracking than speaking formally at a research seminar. Even if you are speaking among a small group of fellow researchers, you will still feel judged. This is natural and is, of course, quite the correct feeling to have. You *are* being judged. You are asking them to judge you: that is the point of the seminar. We are not going to soften this statement by reassuring you that it is only your materials that are being judged or your hypothesis or your conclusions. It is inevitably, to some extent, you, because you are so caught up in your research that you will see it as part of who you are. You will also feel judged because your audience members are, quite deliberately, looking for weaknesses. If you sound hesitant about a method you plan to use, they will be ready to offer an alternative. If you sound anxious about one direction in which your research might go, they will be there to warn you of the dangers ahead or reassure you as to the efficacy of that path.

So, purely for the purposes of helping you, even the most supportive audience at a research seminar will be judging your presentation, considering how best to plug holes in your argument and tease out your hypotheses. Added to that, you will be aware that one or two audience members might know more about your broad field of research than you do, so will be in an excellent position to spot any gaps in your knowledge. It should also be admitted that you might be unlucky enough to have one audience member who simply likes the sound of his or her own voice and delights in pontificating at your expense.

With all of these factors at play, it is not always enough just to keep reminding yourself that this will be, in the end, a positive experience and, on the whole, these people are there to help you. If you look increasingly flustered as the event progresses, you will be making those around you anxious. If you start to look irritated, you will stifle the discussion you need in order to expand your viewpoint. If you look as if you might become distressed by a challenging question or, indeed, any questions, the event will have failed in much of its purpose. Instead, you need to take control.

 EXERCISE 5

Before you can take control, you need to know, as accurately as possible, how you are responding to the situation and how well you are able to assess what is happening. When you next take part in a research seminar, ask a friend to film you (with the permission of all of those involved). After the event, and *before* you watch the film, write down your initial impression of how things went. Here are some questions you might ask.

1   Did I make my points clearly?
2   Was the group supportive of my main points?

3   Did I use visual aids wisely?
4   Was anyone aggressive?
5   Was I defensive? When? Why?
6   Did I accidentally ignore anyone who wanted to ask a question?
7   How many questions was I asked?
8   For how long did I actually think I spoke, both in the presentation and the question and answer section?
9   Was my non-verbal communication (body language) open and positive?

As you make a note of your thoughts on these topics (and you may find others to suit your particular seminar), ask your friend to do the same. Then compare notes, followed by watching the film and seeing who was right. By doing this you will get a good sense of how much you can trust your impressions when you are under pressure. If you discover that this is not a strength, you might want to repeat this process whenever you can in teaching situations in the early stages of your time as an educator.

THE VOICE OF EXPERIENCE

Some experienced academics have likened leading a seminar, or indeed any teaching experience, to conducting an orchestra. One academic expressed it very well:

'To be a good conductor you need to gain the whole orchestra's attention at the beginning, keep the rhythm going, bring in the instruments that need to be heard at particular times, quieting those that might mask the melody, and bring the whole to a satisfactory conclusion at the same time.'

Taking control of a research seminar can be achieved in several ways. If you know that your findings are new and have not been thoroughly verified yet, be open about this. It will not cause any problems at all, but it will keep you from defending a position with material that is not yet robust enough to stand significant scrutiny.

If you have a plan for the material you are presenting, such as transforming it into a journal article, or if it is a draft for a thesis or book chapter, make this clear. This will allow the audience members to make suggestions outside the specifics of the research, touching perhaps on your organisation of the material, how it might best be presented in a chapter and so forth.

If you know that someone in your audience is an expert in a field that overlaps yours or someone there gave you a great idea you are now, with the person's permission, exploiting to the full, acknowledge this. You need to do this even if the person who offered you the idea is your supervisor/mentor. It is difficult to present an argument convincingly if you become aware that one or two members of the group are silently fuming because you did not acknowledge their presence or their help.

If the group is very sociable, and perhaps a little undisciplined, be very firm at the outset as to timing. Give a little time at the beginning for chatting (perhaps arrange a start time that is quarter of an hour before your presentation is due to begin) and then explain that questions will be taken at the end of your talk or you will pause for questions at specific points. The former option is the easier in terms of keeping control, but you might feel that the latter is the better choice for the nature of the topic and either will work as long as you keep control ('We will have time for just five minutes of discussion at points throughout the presentation').

Remember that you want a response from as many members of the group as you can. When you are asked a question, you will obviously be looking at the questioner with interest and, for the first sentence or two of your response, maintain eye contact with just that person, but, as soon as you can, look around and direct your response to the entire group. This shows clearly that you want them all to be involved. In this way you will be encouraging others to add their comments to your response, which could lead to a more general group discussion. When you feel that you have answered the question sufficiently or enough time has been given to a discussion of the point, look back to the original questioner to ask if his or her question has been answered. Doing so will make the questioner feel valued and signal to the rest of the group that you would like to move on.

If you know you have a voluble colleague who will ask a question that runs the risk of being longer than the talk itself, ask another colleague (perhaps your supervisor/mentor) to interrupt if necessary. This will not seem disloyal in you and the questioner is unlikely to take offence as most such questioners have no idea that they are doing this and are happy to be forced into a more concise phrasing of their question.

If you are unlucky enough to have an audience member who is going to ask an unnecessarily awkward or aggressive question, smile politely, tell him or her how interesting you find the question, explain firmly that it is not an area you have considered and add that you would be happy to look into it after the event and get back to him or her. Smile again and look away decisively. You will have the sympathy of the room and someone else will be ready to jump in and reassure you by asking a far more constructive question.

Getting the tone right in a research seminar comes, to some extent, with experience, but they are fluid and spontaneous events, with a variety of purposes working in parallel. As you prepare to present at a research seminar, you might find it comforting to know that even an experienced speaker would go through all of the preparation in this chapter in order to make the most of the event.

TEACHING AND YOUR RESEARCH

You are likely to find that all this preparation has one outcome in particular, no matter what your research area is – it will make you consider your research more deeply from a range of perspectives, some of which you may not have considered before. It will help you focus on what the essence of your research is and why it is interesting. It will help you to express it in a clear and logical way and, in doing so, it may alert you to aspects that need more work and/or further consideration.

Maximising the benefits

There are several reasons for holding research seminars. Universities and other institutions like them because they demonstrate the existence of a vibrant research community. Department managers like them because they foster a spirit of collegiality. Supervisors and mentors like them because they allow them to bring in fellow scholars to support their researchers. Researchers like to attend them because they enjoy the social contact and know that they will pick up some ideas and tips for their research.

None of these points gives you, as the speaker, a reason to like them. You need a compelling reason to be there, because you are the one who is about to put time and effort into the event. Naturally you will get some of the benefits of this social contact, but that is not enough: you are there to gain tangible support for your research and some honing of the skills you will need for teaching.

THE VOICE OF EXPERIENCE

Reflecting back on their first few research seminars, experienced academic colleagues recalled some amazement that others were interested in their (sometimes arcane) topic, some shock at the apparently trivial though occasionally searching questions they were asked and some deep pleasure in the leads and suggestions they were given, encouragement they received and stimulus to thinking that the process provided:

'At first I was surprised to find that, like me, the students seemed to be fascinated by my topics – for instance, I had thought that they might find XXXX [a science proposition] tedious, but they clearly found it exciting.'

(Continued)

(Continued)

'I began to realise that I had to make some explanations clearer to avoid answering lots of basic questions. On the other hand, some students can be scarily perceptive and ask challenging questions – you need to be ready for either; keeps you on your toes!'

'Sometimes I am amazed at the fresh insights they bring to a task or topic – it renews my own interest and can give me fresh enthusiasm and – yes – ideas.'

As we mentioned earlier in our word of warning, this is not a traditional teaching situation, so you need to discover what the group is expecting of you. A full half-hour presentation with slides and handouts would allow you to practise different skills from a ten-minute 'highlights of my research to date' talk. As well as thinking about teaching skills, you will also be concerned to make the most of the occasion from the point of view of your research, so let's break it down a little …

  EXERCISE 6

From the point of view of your research only, tick all of the points below that represent what you hope to achieve.

1   Meet other experts in my area. ☐
2   Show my supervisor/mentor how well I am doing. ☐
3   Get feedback on my research to date. ☐
4   Improve my confidence. ☐
5   Get help with my research methodology. ☐
6   Test the strength of my latest hypothesis. ☐
7   Work out how much research material I need to make a point. ☐
8   Get advice on how to structure my research output. ☐
9   Find inspiration to keep going; discover new research questions. ☐
10   Increase my list of useful contacts. ☐

By considering what you want to achieve you will be more focused in your approach. It could be useful (and would be perfectly acceptable) for you to begin your talk with a plea that reflects one or more of these points – 'I am hoping today to get a sense of whether or not the structure of this draft chapter will work', for example. Your audience will be only too keen to help, so give your fellow scholars the chance to support you.

From the teaching point of view, it is also a good idea to consider in advance what you might gain from the situation. There are two steps in the process. First, beforehand, think about how what you are going to do could translate into a teaching situation. Second, reflect after the event on the extent to which you achieved your goals.

If you are giving a *formal presentation*, you can liken it in your mind to a lecture. There will be differences, in that members of your seminar audience will have broader experience than a group of undergraduates, but they might not necessarily have much more than an undergraduate's knowledge of your specialist area. By working through the checklist and exercise above, you will have considered the level at which to pitch your talk and what you want to get out of it. From the viewpoint of teaching, this situation allows you to learn about:

1   the best time to distribute a handout
2   going through the information given in the handout while making sure that everyone actually has time to read it as you do so
3   making eye contact that is convincing and engaging
4   standing well, moving effectively
5   breathing in a way that supports your voice
6   working from notes rather than a script
7   using teaching aids, such as a data projector
8   controlling, and then using, your nerves
9   pacing your delivery; managing your voice
10   gauging the level of engagement and flexing your talk as necessary.

We will be covering all of these points in Chapter 6, so if you are giving a presentation at a research seminar quite soon, you might want to turn there now to get some immediate guidance.

If you are offering a *brief introduction* to one area of your research, it might feel like the introductory talk you might give at the opening of an undergraduate seminar. It will help you to:

1   make eye contact in a more intimate setting
2   gauge how comfortable everyone feels in a group situation
3   keep an eye on attention levels – watch to see that you are not losing anyone as you progress
4   check if anyone is looking unhappy with your talk or likely to ask questions aggressively.

If you are essentially *leading a discussion*, with the material for this being given out in advance and you simply supporting the discussion with your expert knowledge, this will replicate in many ways the main body of an undergraduate: seminar. You will want to ask yourself the following kinds of questions afterwards:

1 Did I give everyone time to contribute if they wanted to?
2 Did I encourage everyone to contribute, but respect those who did not want to say anything?
3 Did I support the confidence of everyone while still making it clear if I disagreed with a point being made?
4 Did I handle awkward questions well?
5 Did I keep the event on track, keeping to the main points I wanted to cover?
6 Did I leave some 'space for learning' rather than cramming the event with noise and information?

It would be unreasonable to expect of yourself that you could achieve all of your goals in your first couple of research seminars, but if you keep returning to the exercises and checklists in this chapter, you will be able to gauge your progress. You might also like to return to Chapter 2, to the checklist of teaching situations we offered you there, to see if you can try out your teaching skills in those situations, using the suggestions given in this chapter.

THE VOICE OF EXPERIENCE

All of the experienced academics we spoke to recognised that they had taken a long time to become both competent and confident as teachers, even those we would deem to be inspirational teachers. Indeed, several of the latter spoke of still feeling some trepidation before giving important presentations or facing an unusual audience, but they did not see this as a bad thing. Instead, they welcomed the adrenalin rush, feeling that it gave an edge to their performance.

'I don't know if I will ever stop being at least concerned about how well I am doing, if not nervous about it, when faced with a new group or a difficult topic or picky audience – it is performance nerves that we need to ensure that we are at our best … it gives you some zest!"

Usefully there were some suggestions that paying attention to the needs of the audience helped to reduce their own nervous tension to a manageable level.

'Once I realised that they really needed and, indeed, appreciated what I could do to help them understand and survive the system, it helped me to put my own trepidation into some proportion. After all, I have survived and can now help others to do so.'

We have talked here about using this opportunity in terms of your teaching skills, but we cannot leave this chapter without reverting for a moment to the fact that this is a chapter on research seminars and we want you to be able to make the most of the opportunity as a researcher. We offer here some suggestions as to how you might do this.

Remember that networking is no longer just a fashionable buzzword but a vital part of what you need to do to develop, both as a researcher and as an academic. We are not thinking here of cocktail parties or social networking at conferences – you might not be the sort of person who finds that situation comfortable. Instead, we want to cover the basics. Never leave a research seminar without the e-mail address of everyone who has attended. You cannot tell when you might need the help and advice of these people in the future, so make sure you can get hold of them again.

Although a research seminar will give ample opportunity for you to get a response to your research material, you will only get an indirect sense of how well you presented that material. You might contemplate asking a couple of audience members for more direct feedback on your performance. Choose these people with care (you want constructive criticism) and, if you feel brave enough, ask for their thoughts on specific aspects of the talk, such as your voice, your pacing of the points you made and such like.

It is possible for a research seminar to change the whole course of an area of research and you need to be as open as you can to this possibility. We all say that we are open to criticism or new ideas, but most of us also admit to a level of resistance to them ('It will be so much work to change course now', 'I will have to abandon some of my precious material', 'I hate being criticised'). This reluctance to change is natural and, in fact, produces a far more productive situation than sometimes exists for those researchers who change their mind frequently. However, you do need to consider the feedback you get from a seminar with as open a mind as possible, so enlist the help of a friend, a colleague or your mentor/supervisor to go through the experience with you and help you to discern what changes you might need to make as a result.

We mentioned earlier the possibility of reworking material from a research seminar to use in a teaching setting, but remember that it serves other purposes as well. You might be able to work up the material into a journal article or a book chapter or a conference paper – again, talk to your supervisor/mentor about this possibility. Also, do not be put off by one awkward questioner, instead taking an overview of *all* the feedback you were offered when judging how much further use you can make of the material.

TEACHING AND YOUR RESEARCH

It is often the case that challenging questions, whatever their source, will give you cause to wonder if your research is on the right track. Similarly, trying to present your research practice as a logical progression for others to understand and demonstrate the validity and reliability of your findings (or authenticity and robustness of your findings) frequently reveals areas for improvement. Those of us who have been challenged in this way have found, more often than not, that the rethinking and review following such experience leads not to a radical change in the research topic or method, but, rather, an enhanced understanding of the process in which we are engaged and a more thoroughly honed argument to present on future occasions. Each such opportunity leads to better research in terms of your practice and the end product.

As you can see, the actual event is only one part of the process of maximising the opportunity offered by speaking at a research seminar. By considering the event from both a teaching and a research perspective, before and after the occasion, and approaching it in a systematic way, you can gain huge value from the experience and take it forward into the next stage of your teaching and research career.

Four

LEADING AN UNDERGRADUATE SEMINAR

Although we tend to think of the job of teaching, especially at the higher levels of education, as someone standing in front of students giving a lecture, it is far more likely that your teaching career will begin by working with smaller groups and doing far more listening than talking. Seminars are the backbone of teaching at this level, but they can seem like a strange way to teach anyone anything, so we will explore in this chapter what you are supposed to be aiming for and some of the ways in which you can get there.

We should explain first what we mean by an *undergraduate seminar*, as the terminology with which you are familiar might differ from ours. We are referring to a coming together of a group of students (usually between 6 and 16 of them) to discuss one aspect of a course or module, led by one (or occasionally two) tutors. Seminars most usually run alongside lectures and are intended to broaden a lecture topic (or series of topics) by means of discussion. If you are teaching on a distance or open learning course, the seminar may, at least for part of the course, be the only face-to-face teaching the students experience. Indeed, it might take the form of a 'webinar', which would rely on distance meeting technology, such as Skype.

The students in a seminar most usually sit in a circle or scattered around a room, with the seminar leader sitting among them. A seminar leader may give a 'mini-lecture' at the outset, to make sure that, in what follows, the students are all on task, but generally the seminar will be taken up with interactivity. This might take the form of a quiz to test knowledge acquisition or a general discussion or presentations or students working in pairs or groups for some of the time and then feeding back the result of their discussion. The seminar leader will facilitate discussion but not expect to take the lead throughout.

 WORD OF WARNING

If you find that you regularly take the lead throughout seminars – giving, in effect, a series of lectures rather than facilitating discussion – something has probably gone wrong. Maybe the lectures are not giving the students enough information, or they are a nervous bunch, or something about the module is making them unsure or you are giving in to the temptation to lecture when your role is to facilitate. This is very easily done, but, as soon as you are aware that it is happening, you will be able to rectify the situation.

The term 'seminar' is well used in education and has come to mean a variety of things to different people. This in itself might vouch for its value, which is that it allows for variety in teaching and gives students the chance not only to listen to an expert but also voice their own opinions, at least in theory. In practice, you might not feel terribly expert and your students might appear to have nothing to voice, but more on that later.

 TOP TIP

A seminar, as we have defined it above, is also quite regularly called a *tutorial*. Here, we reserve that term to describe another teaching occasion, but do not be put off if what we are referring to as a *seminar* seems to you to be a *tutorial* – or a student study group or a study session – the advice will be valid for all of them.

Before we consider with you some teaching strategies that you could employ in a seminar, we would like to outline what we see as the purpose of most seminars and expand on each a little so that we are working together on similar principles. A seminar is designed to allow:

- students the freedom to express an opinion, even the 'wrong' opinion
- students to ask questions, even the 'wrong' questions
- you to talk through a topic, even the 'wrong' topic
- you to share your expertise, even the 'wrong' expertise.

You might gather from this list that one of the greatest hurdles faced by those without much experience of leading a seminar is the assumption that there are 'right' and 'wrong' things to do. This is rarely the case. If you approach a seminar with the idea that you *have* to cover a list of topic areas, that you *need* to make sure the students have absorbed all of the necessary facts so that they are *fully* ready for an exam, you will always be in danger of lecturing your way through seminars and missing that 'space for learning' about which we are so enthusiastic.

If we take each of these points in turn, we can share with you how 'wrong' can transform into 'perfect', if you let it.

Allow students the freedom to express an opinion, even the 'wrong' opinion

You will find your own style of teaching and, in so doing, find your own way to cope with students who express an opinion or voice an idea that is just plain wrong. Either the student has the facts wrong or the opinion is so wide of the mark you would not feel comfortable allowing it to pass and risk the student (or other seminar members) reiterating the idea in any piece of assessed work. On many occasions, the words 'not quite there yet' could be substituted for the word 'wrong' and, of course, this is a far more positive position for you. If a student were to say, 'It always seems to be raining in that area', you could happily respond with, 'Yes, it does seem that way and there is evidence to bear it out. You will remember from the lecture that …'. In such scenarios honour is served on both sides: the student has voiced a (rather vague and unscientific) opinion and the seminar leader has been able to pounce on it and move towards a firm, substantiated learning point.

However, this is to ignore those really tricky situations when students simply get it wrong. If a student were to say, 'If only World War II had started in the 1930s, they might have been better prepared'. This is a relatively common problem: a factual inaccuracy followed by an unclear opinion. The temptation is to fudge the issue: 'That is an interesting viewpoint; let's explore it together'. It seems as if you have given yourself space to correct the problem without offending the student, but, in fact, you now simply have a student who still believes an inaccurate fact with the remainder of the group of students now being unsure of both the fact and the opinion. You will then spend the next few minutes in a discussion, the sole purpose of which is to try to slip in the fact that World War II did commence in the 1930s and elicit from the student who was meant by 'they' in the original comment.

You do not want to embarrass such students, but neither can you waste valuable learning time in an unproductive discussion based on a false premise, so what do you do? The short answer is that you smile, unembarrassed, and correct the inaccuracy without any particular emphasis and then give the student an option: 'By "they" do you mean the Allies?' (if you want to lead the topic firmly in that direction) or 'By "they", which force do you mean?' (if you are happy for it to go either way). This sounds simple to do, but it takes courage to risk offending the students concerned and it takes belief in what you are trying to achieve to follow through in this way. In practice, students will either accept the correction of the error quietly or they will laugh at themselves for making the mistake.

Thinking about this we realised that most of our students would laugh at themselves and we just reminisced about what lovely students we have shared seminar time with over the years. Of course, then we realised that it could not just be the loveliness of students, we must have been doing something to allow that laughter to happen and this, we think, is the key. Much earlier than the mistake, you need to have started creating a space where learning can happen, yes, but also where mistakes are corrected without embarrassment and opinions are voiced with ease. That is what much of this chapter is about.

THE VOICE OF EXPERIENCE

When you are inexperienced, it can seem much safer to give a lecture, albeit in a small group seminar situation, simply because this places you in authority and reduces the chance of being asked difficult questions or having to cope with correcting students while maintaining their motivation. Yet we are all much more familiar with engaging in a discussion than giving a presentation. Some people find it helpful to reflect on what factors aid social discussion and then try to mimic those in the teaching session.

'I noticed that in a social situation I am quite good at diplomatically correcting a friend or leading the conversation around to a more formally correct viewpoint when it would be rude or hurtful to contradict someone. So I try to bring those skills into my teaching – a relatively new situation, but not that different from what I do in my leisure time.'

Allow students to ask questions, even the 'wrong' questions

In this section, we are not thinking about the wrong type of *factual* question. It might be startling to have a student ask, 'So why has climate change stopped happening?', but you would not find it awkward. Instead, you would be likely to use it as the perfect springboard for what you (and others) might like to say and you could make a mental note to check on the student's progress at some point. Rather, the sort of 'wrong' questions we are think-ing about are those that appear to get in the way of learning: 'Can you remind me, when is the assessed essay for this module due in?' or 'What does that [very basic] term mean again?' or 'Can you tell us a bit more about the module choices for next term?'

So, there you are, having worked hard to prepare a seminar, brimful of ideas you would like to share and wanting to get across a series of facts that you know are important for the assessment, when you are faced with a sea of anxious students, all responding to utterly the wrong question. At first it can be dispiriting: 'Why are they not interested in my seminar?' Often it can be confusing: 'If they keep asking irrelevant questions, I might lose my thread'. Sometimes it can be just plain irritating.

If any of these responses feel familiar, you are not alone, but you have over-looked an important point. If they do not ask these questions of *you*, who *will* they ask? They may have already been given the information but not taken it in, they may have been given support to make module choices or offered exam technique workshops, but all of these are irrelevant at the moment in which they ask that 'wrong' question. They have chosen, either individually or collec-tively, to ask your advice, to give you the opportunity to allay their fears and anxieties. What a compliment.

 EXERCISE 7

Try recording a seminar as you lead it and, as you play back the recording after the event, ignore the general discussion and, instead, focus just on the questions that were asked of you directly. How many did you answer in a way that closed down the discussion? How many did you answer so as to extend a student's query into a discussion? There are no absolute right or wrong answers here. Some questions required a 'closed' answer, but if very few of your responses led to a longer discussion of the point a student raised, you might be veering towards taking too much control of the situation.

You will, naturally, become aware of the 'panicker' and the 'procrastinator', both of whom will lead a seminar astray without a firm hand to guide the occasion, but beyond this you are free to remain true to your purpose. However well planned your seminar, however pressing the deadlines, how-ever fervent your desire to teach them something, they will not be fully receptive to that experience if a large portion of their consciousness is taken up with worrying. Allowing some 'wrong' questions and answering them fully, without resenting the time they are taking up, helps to foster a positive learning environment. It also labels you as an academic who is helpful to students, which will lead to rewarding experiences throughout your career.

THE VOICE OF EXPERIENCE

One of us was reminded recently that our students have lives outside of our teaching rooms and so bring concerns and worries – or even joyful exuberance – in with them. On this occasion, the students arrived for the session having just found out that their group had been chosen to be the lab group to be observed by a prestigious visitor to the university – no amount of somersaults and other attention-grabbing devices were going to get their attention back on to work until they had had an opportunity to get some of their excitement out of the way. The time allowed for this was well spent since otherwise they would have been distracted and fidgety all through the session and everyone would have left disgruntled. The same would apply if some disaster had struck or a fracas could be seen to be going on outside. Sometimes life happens to distract us all and it is wise to deal with it rather than vainly hope it will disappear if we ignore it.

Allow you to talk through a topic, even the 'wrong' topic

A colleague of ours is an incredible educator and yet runs the most peculiar seminars. One of us was lucky enough to be in a seminar group of hers and so saw her in action.

If you go to her office, it is very eclectic, with books in piles around the place, posters on the walls at strange angles, long-forgotten pot plants withering on the windowsill. Despite this appearance of chaos her administrative skills are excellent: relevant handouts are produced for each seminar and one-to-one sessions are frequent and useful.

The seminars open with an easy question being thrown out: 'What do you recall of the lecture on this topic?' or, on her rather more mischievous days, 'Did you find the lecture on this topic to be useful?' Students, lulled each time into a false sense of security despite all previous experience, inevitably hunt through their lecture notes at this point to try to make comment on the main points of the lecture. As the seminar leader, she nods in agreement and makes insightful and useful additions to the lecture points they raise.

After that, anything can happen. She takes intellectual flight, usually carrying a few keen students with her, into realms that are unheard of for the module concerned. For example, a discussion of early novels could easily lead to a discussion of the private family life of Jane Austen; a consideration of a Shakespearean text is rarely abandoned without at least one examination of sexual innuendo and patriarchal society. Whatever it is, it is fascinating. Even students who say nothing at all in her seminars come away having enjoyed the experience.

The point of this diversion is that she appears to do it all wrong, yet it works. Looking back after many years it has gradually become clear: it works because she is completely engaging and is being far more relevant than is obvious at the time. As undergraduates, we saw Jane Austen as a literary icon who must have been a nice spinster, producing 'nice' works for equally nice young ladies: how wrong we were. We were also shocked to find that Shakespearean texts were not altogether decent and, even when we realised it, without her forthright approach we might never have dared to give an example. What she taught us was that art, like life, is complicated and what she encouraged in us is intellectual bravery – a willingness to explore new ways of seeing both art and life.

Of course, she could not run these seminars if she was not certain that others are giving rather more traditional seminars, with orderly discussion and a logical progression through the material. There is room in any institution for both types of educator and you will naturally tend more towards one extreme or the other. Perhaps the ideal is to try to be a mixture of both, following a regular and logical format but allowing for intellectual digressions every now and then.

THE VOICE OF EXPERIENCE

All of our experienced lecturers admitted to having, like us, favourite topics – those issues about which they could talk enthusiastically for hours. If we are lucky enough to have those topics occur within our seminar series, we are faced with another challenge – that of infecting our students with our enthusiasm while resisting the urge to monopolise the talk, which, remember, is at least as much about the students contributing as our role. One of our experienced lecturers suggested that this kind of situation can benefit from prior planning to identify some key aspects of the topic that really engage our attention so we can use them as stimulants to the students and scaffolds for the discussion. Another contributor suggested that teachers should ponder what properties their favourite topics have that might then be identified in topics about which they, and the students, might be less easily enthused. As in our example above, it might be that they are astonishing or controversial or simply an intriguing alternative perspective that can be used to generate debate.

 TOP TIP

It can be useful, if the schedule allows, to leave one or two seminars in a series blank in your planning. Then, if seminars regularly seem to go off topic or questions are asked that you feel

(Continued)

(Continued)

are valid but you are not immediately expert on, you can make a note of these areas. You can then let students know at the time that you will return to their points later. Towards the end of the series, you can then give out a list of the topics/question that you feel require more coverage (be selective) and ask each seminar member to volunteer to give a short presentation on one of the topics in a revision seminar (or seminars) to conclude the series. This gives you time to do a little preparation and it allows them to shine in an area. This is also a good point to ask if they have any additional areas that they would like to add to the list for the revision seminar(s).

Allow you to share your expertise, even the 'wrong' expertise

We all feel comfortable in our own areas of expertise and are likely to be asked to teach broadly in those areas, although 'broadly' here can come to mean 'very broadly' in some instances.

What can be disconcerting in a seminar is if your students throw you off topic. This will be unintentional on their part – they assume you know pretty much everything. If this happens, it is usually a good thing as it reflects their ability to spread their intellectual wings beyond what is directly in front of them, but for you it can be a most uncomfortable experience. The first thing to bear in mind is *all* of your expertise is at their disposal, so an area that might not be your normal avenue of research might be just the one you can help them to follow at this stage in their learning.

This situation needs to be dealt with in two stages. The first stage is to consider the way in which the discussion (or perhaps the questions they are asking) is going. If you feel that it is just too far from the topic of the seminar to be a useful diversion, then you can close it down, neutrally but firmly. If, however, you feel that the discussion and/or questions are going to lead to a useful place, you will want to allow them to happen. In this second stage, two things will occur: you will find expertise that you had no idea you had and you will learn where your 'tipping point' is.

We all tend to label ourselves 'expert' in a few areas and academics are perhaps particularly discouraged from seeing themselves as generalists, yet we do all have a far greater and broader expertise than we acknowledge to ourselves. Thus, when such a situation arises, try to remember what your level of expertise was as an undergraduate and then judge your ability to help and inform your students now based on what you knew when you were in their position. If, having done that, you feel you have reached the point where your expertise really has run out (and this 'tipping point' is one that you will reach surprisingly infrequently), you will need to tell them.

Avoid the temptation to bluff by suggesting that the discussion is becoming irrelevant and you would like to move back to the central topic.

That protects your self-esteem, but crushes a student. Instead, be bold and explain that it is not your area of expertise. Usually this will simply stop the discussion at that point and the seminar will naturally move on, with the members of the seminar knowing the area is one they will have to research independently if they would like to pursue it further. If you feel it would be useful, you also have the option of inviting a pair of students to prepare a seminar presentation on the topic for the next seminar, thus ensuring that they all benefit from the research.

It can make you feel like a failure if you admit to not being an expert on something, but students will not see it that way. They will simply see it as a normal part of the discussion and will be happy to move on. As established academics we judge ourselves far more harshly than our students ever do.

 ## WORD OF WARNING

Students have an uncanny ability to know when you are bluffing. Being caught out perpetrating a bluff just once is enough to lose their trust. They are learning that acquisition of knowledge leads to more questions and they will never be able to know everything. Admitting that there are limits to even your knowledge and expertise can create a positive situation.

THE VOICE OF EXPERIENCE

You will be lucky indeed – perhaps even unique – if you are never asked to lead a seminar on a topic with which you are less than perfectly au fait or never asked a tricky question by a student. It may take a while, but you will come to appreciate that these are opportunities for you to learn with your students. Our team of experienced lecturers made the following observations.

'After all, a seminar should be a joint endeavour in terms of contributions and learning so sometimes you have to mug up on information in advance or check it out afterwards when issues are raised that you are not familiar with.'

'I hope that when I promise to look something up and do so that I am acting as a great role model for the students.'

'When we find in a seminar that no one knows the answer to a question, we all undertake to check it out – it is part of the joint learning situation.'

'I have found asking shy students to find out about something that stumps us all helps them to contribute to the group. It is also a good ploy to give focus to the contributions of a vociferous member of the group.'

Why lead a seminar?

Having shared with you some of our views on the purpose and function of seminars, we should take you back for a moment to consider something rather more basic: why would you want to lead an undergraduate seminar?

We could offer you many reasons here and try to persuade you that you are doing the right thing, but we feel it is more constructive for you to identify your own reasons. You will need to find the motivation to prepare, lead and reflect on your seminars and this takes some thinking about. You will also want to make the most of the opportunity, both professionally and intellectually, so identifying your reasons for doing it makes sense. The checklist we offer you here is not exhaustive, nor is it intended to be an exercise in seeing how many points you can tick off. Rather, it is a range of motivators, some of which will apply you.

 CHECKLIST

1 You need the money and these are sessional (freelance, part-time) seminars. ☐
2 It is part of your contractual obligation. ☐
3 You were asked to lead some seminars. ☐
4 You like a new challenge. ☐
5 You remember good seminar experiences as a student and want to pass that on. ☐
6 You see seminars as the bedrock of teaching. ☐
7 You remember poor seminar experiences as a student and want to rectify
   that, for yourself and/or your students. ☐
8 You enjoy revisiting different areas of your expertise. ☐
9 You want to watch learning in action. ☐
10 You believe it will help you to fulfil a pastoral role. ☐
11 You enjoy the way undergraduates think. ☐
12 You find it satisfying to pass on your knowledge. ☐
13 You enjoy encouraging and controlling group situations. ☐
14 You think you are good at teaching in that situation. ☐
15 You are interested in the views of students. ☐
16 You find lectures too scary to contemplate so would rather stick to seminars. ☐
17 You like to bring a sense of order to a dynamic situation. ☐
18 You see yourself as a natural leader. ☐
19 You like to teach in a relatively informal setting. ☐
20 You do not want always to be the one talking. ☐
21 You think you will find them a relatively easy challenge. ☐
22 You are scared and want to prove that you can overcome the fear and succeed. ☐

You now have a clear understanding of why you are leading – or preparing to lead – undergraduate seminars.

Next, take a moment to consider the reasons that you did *not* tick. These are equally important and being honest with yourself about these now will help you to avoid problems later. There is no judgement attached to this checklist, so, if you have chosen to admit to yourself that you find lectures scary, you should feel reassured that this is a perfectly natural response to a new and rather daunting challenge and help is at hand in this guide. Equally, if you think that seminars will be a relatively easy challenge, good for you. There is enough to challenge us all in academia without every day having to be all about slaying dragons.

On reflection, other choices you have made might give you pause for thought and, perhaps, concern you a little. If you have less than enthusiastically ticked the first three reasons, we hope you have also found others to tick as money, though a significant motivating factor, is not necessarily the most inspiring reason for doing anything in the long term. If you did not even consider placing a tick beside being interested in the views of students, then never mind for now, but you might want to revisit the list in the months to come: we would hope that such an interest would develop as time goes on, as teaching would become rather pallid without it.

 TOP TIP

Employers do love transferable skills. Avoid putting 'leading undergraduate seminars' towards the end of your CV, almost as an afterthought. Instead, analyse what skills you had to deploy in order to be successful as a seminar leader and highlight them in your CV.

Something is conspicuous by its absence from the checklist: your research. While it might be implied in several of the options, it is, in fact, a primary motivating factor for many researchers preparing to lead one or a series of seminars.

TEACHING AND YOUR RESEARCH

During the course of your research you may feel reluctant to include direct references to it in your seminars until you have firm results to disseminate, but bear in mind that research is a process and it will be useful and interesting to your students to learn how

(Continued)

(Continued)

knowledge is generated. It will also be beneficial to you to practise explaining the complexity of your work in terms that enable a relatively lay audience to appreciate that process. For instance, not only might the literature that you have accessed as part of your research be relevant to the seminar topic but also you can impart the skill of searching the literature by including, with guidance, a preparatory or exploratory literature review as part of your seminar series.

Further, it is likely that there will be aspects of your research that have the potential for ambiguity or alternative explanations. You may be convinced that your interpretation is defensible, but be surprised by the perspectives on it expressed by undergraduate or Master's students who are not so embedded in your research paradigm and culture. Ensuing discussions can therefore help you prepare and hone stronger arguments but also give you fresh ideas to consider.

Thus, some of the more generic skills, such as accessing and reviewing literature and generating clear lines of argument, can be used and refined during the course of your teaching, even if the specific topic of your research does not feature in the seminar programme.

Your role as educator

Knowing why you are preparing to lead a seminar group is, of course, only half the journey (albeit the half that is sometimes overlooked). The next obvious question is what on earth are you actually supposed to do?

In some ways this might seem like too obvious a question, begging the response: 'teach them'. In the rest of this chapter, though, we will pick apart this bald statement to consider how you might achieve this deceptively simply goal. First, you might find it useful to consider for a few minutes what it must be like to be on the receiving end of this experience.

Like most graduates, we can vividly recall our first ever undergraduate seminar. One of us was asked, without warning, to read some lines from Chaucer's *Parliament of Fowls* to the seminar group. This was asked of her with an encouraging smile from the seminar leader, with no idea of the number of problems she had just created.

First, this hapless student had never seen a single line of Chaucerian text before. Second, she rapidly realised that, in the original, she could make out very few of the words. Third, she had no idea how to pronounce text from the 1300s and, finally, she was cripplingly shy in front of this new seminar group.

The whole experience, although recalled still with horror, was actually only a momentary lapse of teaching concentration on the part of someone who turned out to be an excellent and inspiring seminar leader, but it was one that has shaped the teaching style of her former student forever.

 ### EXERCISE 8

You might find it useful to recall your first seminar and remember how you felt, how you were made to feel by other members of the group and how you responded to the seminar leader. This is a good memory to capture, store and feed into your approach to leading a seminar.

Moving on from this, you might want to discover at some point how your students feel about the situation you are creating for them. This was recently highlighted for one of the authors when, as part of the preparation for a research project, she asked a group of third-year students how they had felt both in their first lecture and as they approached their first assignment. The words and phrases that came back were startling: shocked, terrified, ill-prepared, stupid, in the wrong place, miserable, confused, angry, embarrassed. The students were not asked specifically how they felt as they sat in their first seminar, but to know that they were carrying this level of negative emotion should be enough to persuade all of us as educators to tread lightly, remaining aware of the social aspects of the situation and the inevitable variation in learning styles in any group.

It may seem strange to be asking you to think of a seminar as a social situation, but of course it is and this has a bearing on how well you can make it work. The fact that we are suggesting 'you can make it work' sounds as if we are placing the onus on you entirely. We recognise that students make it work alongside you, but we also know that you are the lynchpin. We will talk more about this in the section on encouraging discussion later in this chapter.

Learning styles will have an impact on a seminar, as they will in any learning situation. Although we would not suggest that everything you do has to be planned with all of these in mind, it is useful to consider their potential effects in this situation. In the table, we offer you a glance at how this might work.

Although this is a very brief outline of how these learning styles work, it demonstrates that a variety of teaching and learning methods has to be a

Type of learner	Prefers ...	Might ...	Might say ...	Likes you to ...	Would like to ...
Visual	learning by seeing	read a handout while you talk	'I see what you mean'	offer copious notes, use the data projector	write you an essay
Aural/audio	learning by hearing	ignore the handout until later	'I hear what you are saying'	explain things and maintain eye contact	give a presentation
Kinaesthetic	learning by doing	fiddle with the handout	'I get you'	demonstrate how things work, gesture as you talk	give a demonstration

good thing in a seminar. Of course, *you* will also have a learning – and a teaching – style that comes most naturally to you. This will mean that you tend to teach in a certain way, which is not a bad thing. You just need to be conscious of your preferred learning style and allow some variety into your role as educator so all students have at least some access to a learning style that optimises the impact of your teaching for them.

 ## TOP TIP

Your students may not be aware of their own learning style. It can be a useful ice-breaker to ask them to consider how they learn best. Put pictures around the room that reflect different learning styles with the text 'Learning is like ...' above each picture. For example, making bread (this would appeal to kinaesthetic learners), playing the piano (auditory learners) and painting a picture (visual learners). When they enter the room, the students are asked to go the picture that most reflects their view. You then get the chance to explain to them the different learning styles and how they are reflected in the pictures. This will show that you respect how they learn and also give you a useful insight into how you might nuance your style.

 ## WORD OF WARNING

As you become more familiar with your preferred style of teaching, you run the risk of becoming entrenched within that style. It makes sense to work within your own style for much of the time, as this allows you to relax and inspire others, but remain open to the idea that changing your teaching style for some learning events can be challenging and refreshing and will help you to reach all of your learners more effectively.

Setting objectives for seminars

In many structured teaching situations you will be required to set learning aims and objectives. In essence, *aims* are the general goals of a teaching/ learning experience, while *objectives* are more specific, individual learning targets that will lead to the aims being achieved. In a lecture, these can be quite precise as you are in control of much of the situation. In a series of lectures or seminars, you can also be relatively precise as you will have time to alter the teaching and learning parameters later on. In a seminar, there is a greater percentage of free space for learning and this can play havoc with objectives.

While seminars need aims and objectives, you are likely to find that they are not always achieved in every seminar and this is not necessarily a bad thing. You will want to allow space for learning, you need to create a supportive learning atmosphere and you want to respond to specific learning needs as they arise, all of which require you to remain open to objectives that ebb and flow across a seminar series. If you can identify appropriate aims and objectives for a whole series of seminars, you will be in the best position to judge whether or not you have succeeded overall, with the result that you worry less about the odd seminar going astray.

For a series of seminars, you can use the SMART system to assess how well you are achieving the teaching and learning goals you identified at the outset. The SMART system requires that objectives are:

- **s**pecific
- **m**easurable
- **a**ttainable
- **r**elevant
- **t**ime-limited.

In an academic setting, a SMART evaluation could be based on:

- **s**pecific goals linked to the aims and objectives for a module
- **m**easurable outcomes, such as seminar presentations or written assignments
- **a**ttainable objectives based on a collective decision made by colleagues as the module is designed
- **r**elevant outcomes, linked to both the module and the learning programme as a whole
- **t**ime-limited outcomes in the form of a termly essay or similar activity.

The key areas of anxiety for the less experienced seminar leader are likely to be the 'attainable' and the 'time-limited' categories. Achieving the 'attainable' criterion comes with experience, as a result of assessing and reassessing what can be achieved in the time allowed for a seminar and how this might change for different topics, different types of learners, different social mixes.

 EXERCISE 9

One way to get ahead regarding the challenge of attainability is to think back to your time as an undergraduate. Try to recall one particularly memorable series of seminars, a series that you felt was successful in helping you to learn. You could make a note of:

- how many minutes usually elapsed at the outset before the seminar leader called the group to order
- the percentage of time your group tended to spend chatting away from the topic
- how often you were asked to work in groups or pairs
- how much time was spent engaged in an activity, compared to time spent talking on the topic
- the percentage of time usually given over to the seminar leader explaining things while you listened.

Once you have worked through this list, as best you can recall, you will be in a better position to see what is attainable in a seminar, while still allowing it to function effectively as a learning space.

Having a 'time-limited' criterion to work to is crucial, but also potentially painful, because it can mean leaving behind an exercise you thought would be enjoyable and enlightening or abandoning some material that, while not essential to the area under discussion, you think would have been interesting to share. Seminars are about handing over just a little of the control to students, which comes at a price. The benefit of using SMART in relation to a series of seminars is that it forces you to accept that some things have to be abandoned. You are obliged to assess whether or not material is vital and, if it is not, move on firmly when time is pressing.

We have suggested here that SMART can be extremely useful for a series of seminars, but it is perhaps less so for an individual seminar. This is because the criteria potentially work against the aims of a single seminar, stifling out space for learning and the social interaction that fosters it. However, there is an argument to suggest that if you leave the analysis until the end of a seminar series, you are in no position to make changes in the light of your findings. We would suggest that you take a median approach to this by carrying out a SMART analysis for groups of three seminars. In an average term, that would allow you to make two adjustments, if you were to work with a seminar group for the whole time. Of course, if you are going to lead just one seminar, you might want to assess it in this way retrospectively for future reference, always being wary of the potential pitfalls of applying the process to a single seminar.

Aims and objectives are not always easy and often set collectively by colleagues as a module or series of seminars is designed. For seminars, they tend to be flexible and sometimes have to be amended as a dynamic learning situation develops, but they are still a useful means of assessing teaching and learning progress.

Getting the timing right

Let us set the scene. You have a seminar at 2 p.m. that is due to last for an hour and you expect 12 students to be present. The module within which the seminar lies is one of a series of modules called 'Market risk analysis' and you know that there was a lecture this morning.

Your objective in the seminar is for students to come to understand that stock market risk is not always a logical process. It can be predicted to some extent, but predictions need to be based on the assumption that human beings act instinctively and respond emotionally to situations. This is a tricky concept, so you have prepared a series of exercises for the group to work through, in pairs, and you have a handout to support the learning.

Seven minutes into the seminar, when you are coming to the end of your introductory talk, a student asks if what you are saying relates to what was said that morning in the lecture about economic recession being hard to predict. Although you had not aimed to talk about recession, you can see that this could be a useful springboard for getting your point across and so you allow some general discussion to develop. It is too early in the seminar for you to feel that you have lost control of the learning objective – until it becomes clear, nine minutes into the seminar, that very few of the students actually understood the lecture and that they are far more anxious about theories of recession than they are about your detailed thoughts on stock market risk – there is an exam in two weeks and they are all nervous about it.

You calm them down, reassure them that they know more than they think and spend ten minutes recapping theories of recession to restore their confidence. You then give them some website addresses they can visit with useful information on the topic. The computer is a bit slow giving you access to these, so this takes a few extra minutes, but you get there in the end. You are now 22 minutes into the seminar and have not yet touched on your objectives. The whole thing has gone wrong – or has it?

If you assume that the seminar is a disaster, you might be tempted to do one (or more) of three things:

- talk rather loudly and very fast for half an hour so that all of the material is covered
- do the exercises yourself to demonstrate how they would have worked
- despair of your objectives altogether and keep chatting about recession theory.

All of these would give you a learning outcome, but none of them would maximise the benefit of the situation.

If we take a step back, we can see what has been achieved in those first 22 minutes. You have:

- fostered a good relationship with the students – you are now seen as a 'helpful tutor'
- made up for a shortfall in understanding of the lecture that morning, without undermining the colleague who gave the lecture
- helped your students as they begin their revision
- helped them think productively about risk analysis, albeit in relation to recession rather than placing it exactly within your preferred context.

So, you have achieved both teaching and learning so far in this seminar and you can build on that. You simply have to make a decision about what you can still cover – a decision based on your answers to the following questions:

- How excitable are the members of the seminar group? Will they settle down enough to focus on the exercises you prepared?
- Do you need to redirect them away from their tangential subject? Would a few minutes of you talking achieve this?
- Which is the most important of your objectives? How best can you get there?
- Is any of your material time-sensitive, either within a global context or within the context of the module?
- What are the key objectives for formal assessment?

There are quite a few variables to consider here and little time in which to pause and take stock in this way. As you gain experience, you will find it easier to work through this type of teaching dilemma, but in your early seminars you could find it useful to decide in advance what you would leave out if a discussion went in an unexpected direction. To do this, it helps to consider the commonest main components of a seminar.

- **You talking** This will tend to come at the beginning of the seminar, to get things moving. You might naturally expect to give a brief talk at the end of a seminar, to offer a synopsis of what has been learned, but this is not always necessary. It can be equally productive simply to allow the discussion to flow right up until the end of the seminar and let the students leave the room still chatting through the points that were raised.

- **Some written materials prepared by you** This would probably take the form of a handout from a lecture or one you have created especially for the seminar. This is a good way to ensure that, whatever happens to the timing, you will still get some vital teaching points across. However, too great a reliance on a densely packed handout can deaden conversation, which ideally is what each seminar will become. Students can baulk at the formality of a handout and might then simply hide behind it.

 TOP TIP

Use written material as a failsafe. It is useful to include not only materials for discussion but also further references for use after the event. That way, if your timing goes awry you will be less anxious because the students are in possession of the key facts they need. Organisational materials are also useful. Students respond positively to a simple handout at the start of a seminar series that lists your contact details and what you aim to cover in each seminar (ideally, leaving one or two of the later seminars blank or loosely titled at this stage so that you can allow the series to develop naturally).

Some external materials For example, an extract from a primary or secondary source, a demonstration of something in action or an object under examination. This might form the basis of discussion or group work. Its benefit lies chiefly in the curiosity that can be piqued by new materials and the fact that it gives students something very well defined about which to talk. If there is too much, students can become overwhelmed, so choose with care and avoid the temptation to photocopy reams of material on the 'just in case' principle.

 WORD OF WARNING

Make it clear at the outset how much you might reasonably hope to achieve in the time available. If you give students a dozen pages of material or demonstrate six different functions of a piece of equipment, they will become anxious that there is too much to cover. If by the end of the seminar you have

(Continued)

(Continued)

only considered a fraction of the material on offer, they will assume that you cannot judge learning time well or, just as dangerous, they have failed in some way. By opening with an assurance that you are offering them plenty of material for their future benefit, but are only aiming to examine some of it in detail in the seminar allows them to relax and, perhaps surprisingly, this approach seems to make them work harder to get through as much material as possible.

Individual responses to questions from you This is a dream in terms of timing. You control the flow of conversation, you can move it on at will and you can ensure that the timing is never jeopardised. The downside of this is that it is difficult to make the seminar into an intellectually inspiring conversation. Difficult, but not impossible. For some seminar leaders this is the ideal situation and one that they handle brilliantly by allowing not just their own questions but also encouraging other members of the group to ask questions, all under the controlling hand of the leader. It is an art form. It inevitably reduces the freedom of the seminar situation, but this might be a good thing. If your seminars are being overtaken by a very vociferous member of the group or you are struggling to engage a pair of chatty students, then this more rigid approach can work well. It can also be a way of gauging at the outset of a seminar series which are your 'bright sparks' – only the confident tend to speak up in this situation, at least in the first few seminars.

 WORD OF WARNING

If you are taking individual responses to questions as your approach in seminars, remember that some of the students will be visual learners. They will keep their eyes down and be writing up their notes throughout. Do not waste too much seminar time trying to cajole these students into talking. They will talk at some point, but only when they have read all of the written material on offer and made their notes.

Working in pairs or groups to give feedback Pairs of students tend to be easier to keep to time in these situations, so, if you are concerned about the timing but would like to include some group work, putting students into pairs makes sense. Be clear about three things: how long you are giving them to talk before they offer feedback to the group, exactly what you would like them to consider and whether or not you expect all of them to have the chance to feed back to the group. If you tell them at the outset that time might not allow each group to discuss their findings, they will not be disappointed later and will still have achieved the learning even if the group as a whole has not benefited.

TOP TIP

This approach is especially useful if you are running a series of seminars in which you are carrying out essentially the same task each time, such as taking the same type of approach to a series of texts or range of material over the course of the seminar series or taking different approaches but to the same basic type of materials. Students will not lose confidence if not every piece of material is covered in the seminar but will have benefited from working along-side someone else. In these circumstances you will need to make sure you are careful in your calls for feedback to ensure that, over the series, each member of the group has had an equal chance to shine and give feedback.

Student presentations Individual or group presentations are not only a good way to ensure that students become involved in the seminar series but they can also give you an additional opportunity for formal assessment. Presentations make timing relatively easy because you can allocate a certain amount of time for a student or students to present and stress that they need to keep to that time. You can then decide which of the following four options for formatting the discussion would be best:

- Require the presenting students to lead a discussion based on questions they have prepared in advance. This ensures maximum involvement, but be ready to jump in and help.
- Take over yourself at the end of the presentation and lead a discussion based on points covered in the presentation that you would like to explore further. This will allow your students to feel that there is an authoritative voice on the topic in the seminar room.
- Move away from the presentation topic entirely and introduce a new topic for the latter section of the seminar. This gives you the benefit of covering plenty of material, as long as you have time to do it justice.
- Allocate a student or pair of students to lead a discussion on the topic, either independently of the presentation or by preparing their discussion points with the presenters. This gets over the potential problem of students feeling that they only have to be involved in the seminar in which they are presenting and can keep quiet for the rest of the term.

General discussion This is perhaps the most traditional view of what seminars are like – an academic sits among a group of eager students engaged in productive conversation. When it works well it is akin to a sunny afternoon, journeying down a serene river in a boat with a good team of rowers, you with a light hand on the tiller and your students all aiming for the same destination. It is a delight. It happens – often – but always be ready with the approaches we have covered here, just in case your rowing crew is having a bad day.

Encouraging discussion

The guidance we have offered on how to work within the timeframe of a seminar is based on one key assumption: that students will actually talk, to you and/or to each other. This is a huge assumption. You might be the expert in the seminar topic, but students are the undisputed experts in silence. Even the chattiest student on a one-to-one basis can seem quite at ease allowing a gaping silence to develop in a seminar situation. That is why many seminar leaders are delighted if they see a mature student enter the seminar room: mature students are far more likely than younger ones to feel a social obligation to respond to a question.

This brings us back to the social aspect of a seminar. While it is clearly not designed to be a fun social activity (although it can become that), it does require social interaction in a group the members of which might be disparate in terms of their sociability. So, this leads us to the crux of the problem: how *do* you encourage, direct and, at times, curtail discussion?

  TOP TIP

Talking at the outset of a seminar is largely about this social interaction. It gives students the chance to settle down and focus, so even if it is not necessary for you to spend any time introducing the material, it still makes sense to talk for a few minutes just to set the social tone.

THE VOICE OF EXPERIENCE

Looking back over their academic careers, most lecturers we have spoken to recognise that presenting their first few seminar series posed greater, or at least different, challenges from those of more structured presentations such as lectures.

'There is less control over the process and more potential variability in how your aims and objectives will be received and worked on. Those of us who are lifelong researchers as well as teachers have had few research projects go entirely to plan, so coping with the unexpected is a skill we need in both areas.'

'Relatively simple practical obstructions occur whatever your discipline (in one institution, I recall that we had frequent power cuts, which challenged lab work), while the unexpected inaccessibility of resources (bugs, people, those ancient tomes again) challenge resourcefulness and the flexibility of your lesson plan or, indeed, your research design. Most of us eventually recognise that these things are not deliberately conspiring to test our mettle, but are part and parcel of normal academic life.'

The comments above reveal the comforting fact that others have had difficulties with seminars and can provide guidance or share useful strategies. So, next, we are going to provide you with some ideas to help you start to create your personal resource bank of potential responses to common challenges. Then, you can add to it by talking to your peers and senior colleagues about these kinds of issues.

Problems around the amount of talking – or silence – in a seminar are usually fairly easily remedied. However, it is worth remembering that this is the *students'* learning opportunity, so if they choose to remain absolutely silent throughout, it is their right to do so. You cannot become personally offended if they choose not to share your fascination with a particular topic or agitated because silence makes you feel uncomfortable.

Ice-breakers

Ice-breakers are activities that you ask your students to undertake – usually the first time a group meets up – to help everyone get to know each other and bond as a group. Although an ice-breaker is traditionally used with a brand new group, some seminar leaders prefer to leave it until the second seminar. This allows them to decide which ice-breaker might best suit the group and whether or not, in fact, they need to use one at all. If the ice-breaker activity is quite challenging, leaving it until the group members are at least acquainted can pay dividends.

We thought it might be useful to share a few ice-breaker ideas with you. These are simple, not very challenging ice-breakers that would be suitable for use during a first seminar.

- **Pair cards** Each student gets half of a picture card. The students then wander around the room, describing (but not showing) their cards, trying to find 'their pair'. Once they find their partner, they share some information about themselves and make sure to include one trivial piece of information that will help everyone to remember their names. Each person then feeds back his or her partner's information. This is especially useful because it is simple to do and impossible to fail, so nobody will feel daunted by it.

- **Group games** Divide a group into two or three smaller groups and give each group a series of relatively simple, but competitive tasks, such as solving a visual puzzle, resolving an anagram or undertaking a problem solving activity. The competitive edge keeps them going and encourages them to work together as a team. Ideally you will give out enough tasks for each team to win at least once. This can be a lengthy ice-breaker but the time spent is worth it if the group is to be asked to complete more challenging work together on a long term basis in the future.
- **Amazing truths** Create a list of attributes, activities and achievements. Give a copy of the list to each member of the group and ask them to go around and find all the people who fit each description (such as, 'I can ride a bike', 'I can speak Japanese', 'I once climbed a mountain'). Some descriptions will end up with no names beside them, while others will be very popular. This activity encourages plenty of talking and is easy to do, as long as the list you make is inclusive enough for the group.
- **Speed meeting** The members of the group mingle and, as they encounter other people, they have to offer three pieces of information about themselves, such as their names, hobbies and a dislike. This is the least daunting of the ice-breakers in that they then sit down again and you indicate each member of the group in turn, asking for anyone in the group to offer some information about that person.
- **Secret favourites** Put the members of the group into pairs and ask each person to draw an item that means a lot to them (for example, a favourite food item, a pet, a mobile phone). They then have to work back to back with their pair, each taking a turn to describe the image to the other, exactly as it has been drawn on the page, and the other person has to draw the item as they envisage it from the description. The pair then compare the images they have created. This is usually quite a humorous activity and, of course, is also revealing about each person.

Ice-breakers are risky things: they can work absolutely brilliantly and bring a group together with very little effort or fall flat. The risk is dependent on both the type of person you are and the students in the group. You cannot dictate the types of students you will get in a group and we do not think it is possible to tell which groups will respond well or poorly to an ice-breaker, so it is down to you to do all that you can to make it work. If you appear hesitant or nervous, then it might have the opposite effect to that desired, with your students feeling uncomfortable rather than socially reassured. If you appear to be confident that the ice-breaker will actually break the ice and get things moving socially, you are more likely to succeed.

 EXERCISE 10

Ice-breakers are a little like good recipes: you hear of one and instantly forget the detail; then you want to try cooking something new and how to make it niggles in your brain. You could use the space given here to record just a few key details of ice-breakers you have experienced or heard about, so that you have an ice-breaker 'recipe bank' waiting for you, with just the right one for each occasion.

....

....

....

....

....

....

....

....

Ice-breakers, however effective, can only do so much. With that in mind, here are some remedies for difficult situations that have worked for us over the years.

The entire group is resistant to talking

- Let them talk to each other rather than you. For example, introduce some group work until they become more used to their voices in the room.
- You may have a group predominated by visual leaners. If this seems to be the case, try introducing more written material.
- Begin with one student who will make eye contact with you, but do not rely on a duologue; open it out as soon as you can.

The atmosphere is oppressive; the students seem resentful

- Do not ignore this natural social cue. In the first instance, comment that they seem quieter than usual and simply ask if they are especially tired or finding the course difficult. This works more often than you might expect and you will find that they were just waiting for the chance to tell you what is worrying them.
- If you have set up presentation groups, one unhelpful member of that group can cause resentment that spreads, so look for clues around this and tackle it after the seminar with the presentation group.
- Check with academic and administrative colleagues – has something happened about which the group members will need reassurance next time you see them?

One keen student is taking over the whole discussion

- Allow this to happen for a little while. You might just have hit on an area about which he or she is especially knowledgeable and normality will return soon enough.
- If it continues and it is a mature student, have a quiet word after the seminar, saying how much you are enjoying the two-way conversation, but that you both should probably give the others a chance. The social impetus that led the mature student to speak up will also ensure that he or she is unlikely to take offence.

- If it is not a mature student, it is usually best dealt with in the group. Other students will be resentful of one student taking the limelight, so they will support your move to curtail the situation. Allow the voluble student to make a point and then ask another student to comment on it. If you comment, you will be encouraging a two-way conversation with the talkative student, so opening up the discussion in a targeted way is far better.

A normally enthusiastic student has gone quiet

- It is tempting to rely on the goodwill and enthusiasm of one or two students who are always happy to respond, then feel upset or confused when one of them refuses to meet your eye and is silent. The answer is to do nothing for the first seminar in which this happens. Just look for clues: perhaps the student is unwell or has had an upsetting time beforehand.
- If the silence continues and the student is involved in a group activity for the series, such as preparing a group presentation, ask the whole seminar group how things are going with their preparations, to try to gauge if there is a problem there.
- If there is no obvious reason for the silence, find any excuse to reach out to the student. Vague 'How are you?' questions might not help here. Instead, find a question that relates to an earlier interaction and use this as a reason to strike up a conversation at the end of a seminar.

THE VOICE OF EXPERIENCE

For all of the challenges noted above, it is worth considering how much the physical environment is influencing the process. If at all possible – bearing in mind the strange and wondrous ways in which room bookings are made in universities – try to ensure that the size of the room and its general nature complements the number in the group and the nature of the task. One experienced colleague recently moaned to us:

'To state the obvious, a large, raked lecture theatre for a seminar of eight to ten people is not conducive to collegiate discussion – what would be better would be a medium-sized room with a round table. It can take a lot of time and energy to convince our room bookings people to grasp that and even then they often can't do anything about it.'

Even if your influence with 'room bookings' is not strong, you can influence the layout and signals sent about the nature of the interaction. For instance, once colleague suggested:

'If the better option of a flat room with moveable furniture is not available, you can ask the students to sit in the centre of the first row or two of lecture seats and 'acquire' a few chairs from a neighbouring room to face them or encourage them to sit with you in a more circular array, turning to the side or around as necessary to maintain eye level and eye contact. You need to be in charge of the furniture, not the reverse.'

Another pointed out that an important consideration is where you distribute different kinds of students in the space you end up with:

'A dominating or vociferous student gains less attention if not centre stage but seated next to the tutor, while a nervous student can be encouraged to participate more if in easy eye contact with a sympathetic tutor. If you have a rectangular table, you might sit on one long side to increase the sense of democracy, but it is a good idea to be alert to dominant students taking the "head of the table".'

You keep running out of time to cover your material

- You need to take stock, as in the example we offered earlier in this chapter. It may well be that you are achieving what is needed simply by discussion rather than working through all your prepared material.
- If you feel general chatting is getting in the way, revert to whole-group discussion or a mini-lecture for ten minutes so as to regain focus.
- If you feel intellectual but tangential talking is getting in the way of your learning outcomes, check first that your learning outcomes are SMART. If you do not need to change your learning outcomes, change the situation by moving to small-group work with well-defined areas for discussion prior to giving feedback.

You keep running out of material

- This is less likely to happen and if, on just one or two occasions, you run out of prepared material and have to ad lib your way through, it will not be a problem for you. Indeed, many experienced academics happily run success-ful seminars with almost no prepared material.
- If it is making you anxious, do not give in to the immediate temptation simply to add more material. Instead, consider for a moment if you are working the material hard enough. You could, for example, be asking for a superficial general discussion when what is needed is more in-depth analysis. Confidence is needed to push material as far as it can go in a seminar situ-ation, which comes with experience – as long as you avoid cramming seminars too full at this stage.
- If you conclude that you do need more material and present swathes of writ-ten material to a seminar group more used to a two-page handout, students may feel that they have failed. Seminar groups are more sensitive than you might expect and are susceptible to assuming that they have done something wrong when you change your way of doing things. You will need to be positive and reassuring if you make this change.

There is one final issue to discuss before we leave this chapter: how much of yourself to put into a seminar. By this we mean how much are you prepared to reveal? Many academics will remember seminar leaders from their days as students, some of whom took them as chiefly social occasions, discussing every aspect of their lives and leaving scant space for academic pursuits. They will also remember others who revealed nothing of themselves at all and whose teaching was robotic and aloof. Clearly a middle ground needs to be achieved.

The students think of you as a leader, an expert in your field who will guide them through the journey ahead. So, revealing your own initial response to the material under discussion – even if this seems to expose a weakness – is not going to be a problem; instead, it will be one of the many ways by which you can connect with the group. Similarly, if you are asked an offbeat question to which you do not know the answer, it is not going to cause the group anxiety if you admit this and offer to e-mail the answer later in the day to the whole group. The secret is not to be unrevealing, but, rather, remain aware at all times that you are the leader, sharing the group's confidence in your abilities.

THE VOICE OF STUDENT EXPERIENCE

It was not only experienced *academics* with whom we talked in preparing this guide; we wanted you to hear the voices of experienced *students*, too. This is how some of the students said they feel in seminars.

'I feel like I am a real part of the university, not just one in a sea of faces.'

'It is my chance to contribute my ideas, to try them out in safety, though I would never dare offer a view in a lecture.'

'Sometimes I wish we didn't have them when they are just chat-shops with no obvious purpose, then I am in a really lively one with lots of debate with a focus and I wish we had more like that.'

'The tutors seem more human and approachable in seminars so I feel like I want to do well to please them.'

'I prefer the ones that we have to prepare something for or read up in advance – then I know what to expect and don't get caught out looking stupid.'

'It feels like the subjects are easier to grasp because they are broken into bite-size pieces and you can ask questions.'

'This is what I call proper learning – its active and sometimes good fun, not dry old stuff being pushed at you or over your head.'

Five
DYNAMIC LEARNING ENVIRONMENTS

In this chapter we will be returning to small-group teaching, but, unlike seminars, we are thinking here of teaching situations where the dynamics are more fluid than a seminar and the learning often takes place through action – that of the academic or the students or both. We would include in this broad definition, for example, laboratory work, field trips, tutorials and skills workshops. We will be covering tutorials in detail in Chapter 8, but the principles we advocate in this chapter apply to all of these examples.

By 'small', in this instance, we have in our minds a group of about six to ten students. This should be the number to aim for at first. When you are much more experienced, you may find that you can achieve the same outcomes with groups of up to 15, even 20, but, despite experience and confidence, this can be extremely demanding and some students may feel that your attention is too diluted by being given to so many.

The teaching techniques we discuss throughout the rest of this guide do apply to some aspects of small-group teaching, but it also raises its own challenges and these are what we will consider here.

Preparing your material

 WORD OF WARNING

Ensure that you remain aware of the imperative to consider the special educational needs of *all* of your learners as you prepare for any learning event. In the case of dynamic learning environments, you must pay particular attention to those whose hearing is diminished in any way and those who have difficulty concentrating in noisy environments. Further, you have another category

(Continued)

(Continued)

to consider: those who are learning in a language other than their first language. In some cases, it might be their fourth or fifth language, so you need to take this into account if some of your students are in this position. A learning situation in which everyone is shouting and/or gabbling at each other might be a hindrance to these students. Although shouting and gabbling can be productive, make sure that there are also lulls in the activity for 'catch-up' time, some small-group or pair work tasks and plenty of written materials to take away.

To some extent, the material you choose for this situation will naturally depend on the learning needs of your students, your research interests and the overall requirements of the course or module. Beyond this, here are some guidelines you might want to follow.

Supportive, not overwhelming, material

The idea behind small-group teaching of this sort is that the learning situation evolves during the event. This leaves many of the spaces for learning that we talk about throughout the book. While they are thus exciting teaching environments, they can also be challenging.

If you are not very familiar with teaching in this situation, there is a temptation to control it. The first way in which most academics would attempt to do this would be to overwhelm the situation with far too much material. We have seen this happen: the group session ends up playing out like a seminar or, at worst, like a mini-lecture for a small audience.

Telling you this is not necessarily going to make you cut down your material to a reasonable amount for the situation, so we would suggest a two-pronged approach. Look at your teaching aims and objectives for the session, plan the activities you aim to include, then (and only then) write up the material you can include. You might then create any of the teaching aids we considered earlier.

Once you have prepared the material, take the second step and produce more material on a 'just in case' basis. Just in case they are a quiet group of students or you have misjudged the timing or one of the scientific experiments you aim to use goes wrong or one of your demonstrations fails. This extra material must be kept separate from your 'core' material, but can be whipped out at a moment's notice if you need it. Chances are you will not need it, but it will have helped your confidence to have it beside you during the session.

Dynamic, not static, material

The point of a dynamic learning environment is, obviously, that it remains dynamic rather than becoming static. For this to happen, you must pass over to the students even more control than you would in a seminar. We see ourselves in this situation as providing a framework, solid but sparse, within which our students can learn. Any teaching material that suggests there is one 'proper' way to do things is likely to close down the space for learning and so we keep the telling of 'rules' of the subject to a minimum and, instead, choose material that allows students to discover the rules for themselves or question the rules they thought were there.

We would also reduce to a minimum material that requires students to be physically static. A screen with information on it requires a group to sit or stand still and look at it; a handout requires the time to keep still and read. We do use both of these teaching aids (and others), but work them into the situation. So, for example, we would give a handout at the beginning, for students to read as we set up the equipment, or at the very end as a 'take away' resource. We would use a smartboard or whiteboard and a flipchart, but only briefly, and ensure that a blank slide is shown during times of activity, so as not to distract the students.

 EXERCISE 11

Some people are very good at giving simple, clear instructions; others really struggle in this area. The problem is that it can be difficult to tell which type of person you are in a dynamic learning situation. Were you unclear or was the situation just too noisy or were your students too boisterous to be listening to you properly? If you are unsure about how well you do in this area, try giving the instructions you aim to give in a dynamic learning situation to a group of friends before the event. Then ask them to write down what they think you mean. Ideally, you will want to do this in a social setting where people are happily chatting to each other as they often will be in a learning environment of this type. When you compare what you thought you said with what they thought they were meant to be doing, it will become very clear whether your instructions were workable or not. If you do not feel secure about giving good instructions, always make sure that you offer back-up written instructions or walk around each group asking the students to confirm what they are planning to do.

Student-produced material

One of the several reasons for needing to introduce only a relatively small amount of material into a dynamic learning environment is that the students will be creating their own learning material. A group of students working on a wiki, for example, might ask for your guidance, but will then continue to produce material that will reflect their own immediate learning and, perhaps, also support students in other groups. A group carrying out an experiment might need your help only in the early stages, before they then move on to create their own learning.

This is not always easy. How far can you let them go wrong before you step in? Is going wrong useful to the learning? If they are using the 'wrong method' will it still get them to the 'right' place? At what point should you intervene and how? These are decisions you make on the spot and they are not always straightforward, but come with practice. So, in your first few small-group sessions you will probably get this wrong, but it will not matter too much. At that stage you will be finding your way and still have created some space for learning and shared some of your expertise. The key is to forge ahead, knowing that you will improve hugely with each session, as long as you bear in mind your goals and the advice we offer here.

 WORD OF WARNING

While students enjoy becoming involved in activities and will happily give their best, they become thoroughly irritated if they begin to suspect that *all* of the input is to be theirs. They feel that this is too much a case of 'the blind leading the blind'. They expect material and teaching from you, so make sure that they always feel the encounter has offered value for their time and effort.

As you can see, preparing material for this type of situation needs a delicate hand. We try to think of it as offering them the material that makes the rules of the game clear, but does not actually play the game for them.

THE VOICE OF EXPERIENCE

When discussing activities in sessions, we were reminded by colleagues how really important it is that your instructions about any activity in which you would like the students to engage are clear and unambiguous. Otherwise your and the students' time will be wasted sorting out misconceptions or arguments between group participants. You can check for yourself any implicit assumptions you may be making about prior learning, skills or experience, but some colleagues said that it is helpful, when you are preparing to run workshop-type sessions, to ask a friend or colleague to read the instructions you have drawn up, then tell you what they think you intend to happen.

Judging and balancing time

One feature of dynamic learning situations is that they often take up more time than lectures and seminars. It would not be unusual to run a whole-day workshop on a topic or set of skills or to expect your students to spend a whole morning on one laboratory session. This means that you have more time at your disposal than usual, which is exciting but also, of course, you have more time to try to control, which will be a challenge.

We have implied a couple of times that it can be useful to watch other educators at work in specific situations. For a dynamic learning environment, we think it is highly important to have a good sense of what others are doing. This might not always involve witnessing a session in action – colleagues can talk through their sessions so as to give you a good sense of what they entail – but, as much as you can, we would say 'look and learn'. Your learning might be based on admiration of a colleague's style or having seen a colleague teach in a way that you know would *not* suit your topic or your personal teaching approach: either is useful in helping you to get a feel for how to make the most of this teaching and learning opportunity.

You might naturally suppose that working in a laboratory setting would provide the exception to this advice. After all, you have spent many years in a laboratory, so it should be second nature to you to teach in that dynamic learning environment. Not so. Being the academic rather than the student is a radical shift, so take the opportunity to shadow a lecturer if you can so that you can gain the new perspective you need.

THE VOICE OF EXPERIENCE

Reflecting back on our own experience as students, one of us had not realised just how much lab work was aided or facilitated by lab technicians and research assistants. On metamorphosing into a teacher, it took some time to learn the institutional culture regarding the remits of the different roles because of fear of 'bothering people'. She found out by trial and error that it is all too easy to try to be independent and end up treading on toes, either by demanding too much or demanding too little of those others who work in the lab. By far the best route to fitting in is simply to ask what balance other lecturers have between doing things themselves and asking others to help and then talk to the helpers themselves about what they would prefer. One of our science colleagues did warn, though:

'Be prepared to negotiate your own role, making it clear that, in this instance, you are seeking support for your teaching duties rather than for your own research – different levels and kinds of help might be available for the two different roles in any particular culture. Some of our technicians are kind and easily put upon, while others need to know chapter and verse that it is part of their job and not yours.'

The problem with timing is that it fluctuates so unpredictably during a small-group session, particularly if you have specific aims in mind. There are several causes of this:

- you become involved, lose track of what you were aiming to achieve and suddenly find that the end of the session is near
- an activity that, in prospect, seemed to you to be quite easy takes far longer than you had anticipated
- the students love what they are doing and become totally engrossed so that you struggle to call them to order
- they want to take the session to learning places you had not expected to visit.

When you review this list you will see that all of these are positive scenarios, reflecting active learning and good student engagement. Even the point about students finding it harder to do something than you had anticipated shows your planning was slightly out rather than that anything was going wrong with the session.

Of course, it is easy for us to point out the positive side of all of these situations. The negative side is that you will be working to a syllabus and need to fulfil the learning aims and objectives of a module. Somehow you have to retain sufficient control over the time so that the necessary learning takes place, but allow enough fluidity for the situation to remain dynamic. Again, we know that this comes with practice, but, in the meantime, there are techniques you can use to support what you are trying to do.

Try to avoid revealing your entire plan

Although students will want to know the 'rules of the game' and be given a structure within which to work, you do not need to list *all* of the learning points you are hoping to cover. Either offer just a few of your main points to get them started, so that they have a rough idea of where you are all going, or give them a brief overview of what you are aiming to achieve. If you do this, you can have more detailed points ready – one per data projector slide, for example – so that you can reveal them during the session only if you know you will have time to achieve them. In this way, students are given the security of a learning structure without feeling that they have failed or missed out if you do not reach the end.

 WORD OF WARNING

If those who lead dynamic learning events do not reveal their entire plan at the beginning of the event, they seem sometimes to be gripped with the irresistible urge to smile archly at students and say, 'but more of that later' or some such phrase, making it clear that they are in control of the event. We have noticed that this often seems to encourage a whole series of meaningful stares and pregnant pauses, as if the academic is a conjuror about to reveal a magic trick or a mindreader who can penetrate the recesses of any student consciousness. Please try to avoid taking this approach at all costs – students will simply waste time speculating.

In a lab setting, the experience with one group of students will not necessarily enable you to predict exactly what will happen with the next group conducting the same practical work. Logically this should be the case, but there are even more variables in a lab than there are in a workshop situation. You are balancing giving out information with student-led information gathering and you are doing it in a setting that is, by its very nature, open to variations in timing. It is interesting to see how the timings for the 'same' practical work can vary so much and assessing why this has happened can sometimes throw up useful teaching pointers.

THE VOICE OF EXPERIENCE

It can be particularly disconcerting if you have several small subgroups, each working on a task simultaneously, and one or more groups finish it much more quickly than the others. Our experienced colleagues confirmed that this is another instance of it being useful to have another small activity up your sleeve just in case those groups become noisy or look very bored (most often they will just enjoy talking quietly among themselves). However, one of the academics raised a particularly good point:

'It should not be a new activity that the remaining groups will regret missing out on. Instead, it should be a simple elaboration of the first task.'

Use breaks to control time

Students instinctively use breaks as a way of consolidating their learning processes. Even if they are chatting to others during a break, they are still cogitating on what they have learnt and mentally preparing to assimilate the next lot of information. That is why breaks make a natural 'firebreak' between one section of a small-group workshop and the next. If students are told that you hope to cover a certain area of activity by breaktime, they will naturally try to achieve this.

TOP TIP

It can be a good idea to plan your schedule around rather longer breaktimes than normal. If, for example, you plan for 20-minute breaks during the session, it is easy enough to ask your students to return in 10 if you find you are running out of time. We would not advocate this as the epitome of best practice, but it does give out the message that things need to run a little faster on their return.

Handouts leave you carefree

Well, to some extent they do. If you have put all of the vital learning points on a handout ready to give to students at the end of the session, you can at least relax a little, knowing that if the small–group session becomes more dynamic than you had expected your students will still be given all of the information that they need, even if there has not been time for them to put each point into practice.

 TOP TIP

If you will be going on a field trip and there will be handouts that have been produced by an external body (a guided tour of an exhibition, for example), it makes sense to ask for copies of these in advance and produce a supplementary handout if you need to in order to cover your aims and objectives. If you cannot do this ahead of the trip, you might like to scan the handout so that in your next session with the group you can show the handout on an interactive whiteboard and the group can supplement it with their learning points from the trip. The new version of the handout can then be saved and distributed.

Field trips used to be undertaken, in the main, by a group of students and academics travelling together to a venue and so having an extended learning experience. Nowadays it is as likely that everyone will make their own way to a venue, meet there and disperse straight after the learning event. If the expense or timing makes shared travel impractical for the group, think about creating either a wiki (if the event is a major part of the module) or an online polling space (if it is a more minor learning event) so that students can share their immediate responses afterwards as well as their more considered views later. You can then use this resource as one of your teaching aids in the next learning event.

You will note that our focus here has been on the potential problem of running out of time and we recognise that this aspect of a dynamic learning environment will be greater or lesser depending on your objectives for the session. We have failed, so far, to mention the possibility of running under time and being left with a group of students who want to be active learners but to whom you can offer no activities. This is because it happens so rarely, but, if it does happen to you, here are some simple remedies.

- Revert to a less dynamic mode. For a moment, think of the group as if the students were taking part in a seminar and simply ask them their opinions and generate discussion rather than relying on activities.
- If you have some reserve material, this is the time to use it. Some academics will hold back reserve material that has been designed to be relevant to the module as a whole rather than just one or two sessions, so that they have some useful back-up material whenever it is needed.
- Improvise! You are the expert in the field and students will enjoy listening to you talk about your research progress for a while, especially if you are revealing material that is not going to be included later in the course.
- You could offer some instruction in research methods, revealing perhaps how you have done (or are doing) things and talking with the students about how this might relate to their work.
- If you only have ten minutes to go when they come to a natural endpoint, try being bold and just let them go early. They will appreciate the 'reward' of their hard work being recognised and the slightly longer break before their next learning event.

WORD OF WARNING

Part of being in control of the situation is making judgements about, for example, whether or not students could leave a little earlier than normal and whether or not to revert to a more general, relaxed discussion if you have run through the activities you had planned. This is to the good, but make sure that it is an occasional choice you have to make. If students come to expect that you will not push them too hard or keep them to the end of the session, they can become resentful when you revert back to the normal way of doing things.

TEACHING AND YOUR RESEARCH

Planning for a dynamic learning event is, in many ways, akin to planning your research for a doctorate. There is a time limit and some guidance available about how long certain contributing activities might generally take, but the unexpected happens with a regularity that surprises novices though not experienced researchers. Therefore, any plan, whether for a PhD or a dynamic learning event, must incorporate some room not just for flexibility but also creativity. Any practice in dealing with unexpected challenges and drawing on your own creativity helps you develop as a researcher. Similarly, managing groups of people with different abilities and temperaments through activities is a skill that will come in handy as your professional career develops.

Structuring your aims and objectives

Given that we have spent much of this chapter focusing on the fluidity and dynamism of this type of learning environment, you might suppose that your aims and objectives would need to be equally fluid, but this is not the case. Indeed, your aims and objectives need to be quite as firm as they are in any learning situation. In workshops around skills training, for example, you might be aiming to cover a very lengthy list of specific objectives.

This might seem to create a paradox – specific objectives in a dynamic environment. Solving the riddle is possible; it just takes some creative thinking. In a dynamic learning environment, the learning objectives might be met in an easily evidenced way. If, for example, you are giving a session on voice coaching and part of the learning is breath control, you can demonstrate a breathing technique, ask the students to practise it and then assess whether or not they have mastered the technique. This is frequently the case in small-group learning – assessment is immediate rather than deferred. This brings the benefit of allowing you to evidence that your learning aims have been met as you go along and adapt them if necessary to a changing situation.

THE VOICE OF EXPERIENCE

Remember that formative as well as summative assessment should be part of your teaching in this situation as well as in more formal teaching sessions. Our student respondents alerted us to one thing that annoys participants in learning activities: being unsure if what they have produced is what is needed and, indeed, if other groups have produced something similar or different. They suggested that lecturers should not forget to include feedback in a plenary session in their planning for smaller groups, giving a summary of the results of their labours, even if they have checked with each one that they have reached the intended goal. We would add from our own experience that it is worthwhile including in your instructions the requirement that they elect at the beginning of the task the person charged with feeding back so that one person can make notes as they go along in preparation.

The secret to success in this area is to create a balance between working towards specific learning objectives and more general but equally productive learning. The rationale for this is that you need to create a balance of intensity and students need to learn more than just specific objectives. In this situation, they are also learning to work within their peer group, negotiate, regarding time and space, whose turn it is to summarise the group product and feedback, as well as how to use resources effectively and sharpen their independent research skills as autonomous learners. We think of this learning as *buffer learning* – that is, it provides a buffer between the requirements of teaching and learning objectives and the demands of a dynamic learning situation. There will be more or less buffer learning from session to session, but it will always be there; it is part of what takes place in the space for learning that you are creating for your students.

 EXERCISE 12

For your next dynamic learning situation, list your specific learning objectives.

In what activities will your students be engaged?

How will you judge what they have learned?

Which of the objectives could you drop from the session if you have to?

What teaching aids will support your work with the students?

What 'buffer learning' will you expect to see?

It is a good idea to work through this exercise as you deliver a series of several dynamic learning situations so that you can evaluate how your teaching style is developing and how the series is progressing.

A series of dynamic learning events

One of the pleasures of dynamic learning events is that they often tend to form part of a continuum of learning on a topic over a lengthy period. Whereas lectures and seminars are often predicated on the principle of 'learn and move on', workshops, lab work and other dynamic learning events are a more flexible part of a whole. That is because what is learned in one session is re-established in the next, missed opportunities are recaptured in later events and learning in different aspects of the subject area will take place at varying rates across time.

This puts you in an enviable teaching position: you will have learning objectives for an event and these will work within the aims of a course or module as a whole, but you will not (as you might in a lecture) need to feel panic rising towards the end of the session. Any expected learning that you hoped to achieve can be delayed until the next session. Of course you will not want to be forced to cram the last few sessions in a series with too much material or too many objectives because then you might have no choice but to lecture the students, though you will still have some leeway.

 TOP TIP

Using online resources (wikis, online polling, virtual learning environments, social networks, image-sharing resources and so on) to extend and enrich the learning beyond each immediate learning event can be of significant benefit in a dynamic learning environment. Just make sure that if the system you set up results in students sharing their material, either from group to group or from one year's cohort to the next, that they are aware that their intellectual property is going to be used in this way. In our experience, students are excited and flattered by this prospect, as long as they are informed at the beginning of the course so that they know what is going to happen to their work.

Although the situation is so fluid, students often like to grasp the sense of structure that comes with you dictating the pace and style of teaching and learning and this can be achieved to good effect in a series of events. You can decide in advance of each event how much you are prepared to stand back and how much direct teaching will take place. You can then use this to form a pattern that students will recognise and respond to positively. You might, for example, explain at the outset of a series that:

- you intend to talk to them for the first 20 minutes of each session
- then move on to activities for much of the rest of the session, before
- bringing them together to feed back their findings before the tea break, after which they will
- continue to work in groups, putting their findings into practice, so that they can
- demonstrate their newly acquired skills towards the end, leaving time for you to
- control the last few minutes so they leave the room with you having summed up the shared experience for them and set the agenda for the next session.

There can be a temptation in lab work to shy away from the last two parts of this outline. Scientific results are not always easily demonstrable in a few minutes and, if a group is split into a several smaller groups for the session, you might be concerned about the time this would take. We have seen this potential problem overcome by students being given a questionnaire about what they have achieved and then each group feeding back its answers to just one or two of the questions. If this is not possible, then you have to be the one to give a broad overview of what has been achieved. This is preferable to letting the students leave the lab at the end of the session with little sense of their having completed the learning event.

 ### WORD OF WARNING

In a lecture, you can assume that students are 'getting it'; in a seminar you can move students quite firmly towards 'getting it'; in a dynamic learning environment, when you are allowing students to voice their own opinions in a relatively unmediated way and show off their skills at any level, you are risking becoming irritated or despondent. When you read the online comments about a learning event or see your students try out a clearly false premise, try not to judge them by your standards. They do not have your level of knowledge and experience, so will make naïve comments that disappoint you – just as you would have done at their stage of learning.

Techniques for encouraging engagement

It may be obvious from the rest of this chapter that the first principle of encouraging engagement is to be clear – about what it going to be learned, about what students are expected to do and about why this dynamic learning situation is taking place.

 ### WORD OF WARNING

Although we will be stressing the value of engagement in this section, we would not want to confuse 'engagement' with 'learning'. For a plethora of good reasons, some students might not want to 'join in' very dynamically, but this does not mean that they are not learning. Although you will want to encourage everyone to have an equal chance to contribute, judge your success as an educator by what everyone has learnt, not by how active they all were. Space for learning often happens in quietude.

Sharing the chairing

If your dynamic learning environment involves students spending some time sitting around discussing an aspect of the area under review, try not to assume that you will always be the one to lead the discussion. Instead, try nominating individual students (or pairs of students) in advance, letting them know that in a particular week they will be expected to chair the discussion.

If group discussions are likely to take place in smaller groups on a regular basis, such as in a series of workshops, you could suggest that members of the group take it in turns either to chair the discussion or give a presentation of a few minutes so as to explain their findings or describe their progress.

Brainstorming

Standing beside a board and asking students to throw ideas at you about how to proceed with a project or share how they would approach a problem is one way to encourage 'no responsibility input' or ask for creative as well as obviously practical solutions. By suggesting an idea in this situation, contributors are not saying that they have the correct or only answer to a problem or they know the best way forward – you are all just sharing ideas. Even the quiet students tend to feel comfortable about speaking up in this situation and giving an encouraging smile to a quiet student will often produce a pleasing result.

Learning needs analysis

Although a full learning needs analysis might be too burdensome to tempt you to use it simply in order to encourage involvement, a brief version of the process can prove useful. Students usually respond better if they know they have been noticed and if they feel that their needs are being considered. This need not be a task for you – you could prepare a questionnaire and ask members of the group to work in pairs and elicit the information from each other. They can then be encouraged in each session to reflect on how they could address their needs.

We have seen this technique used effectively by means of the creation of a learning journal that is completed in the course of a series of dynamic learning events, with students being asked to produce a short report at the end in which they outline their initial learning needs and analyse how well they managed to nuance the activities to support those needs. They will, of course be reflecting in part on how well you designed the course, but the onus is on the students to be active in their learning journey.

Skills inventory

This is another technique that can be a powerful learning tool without especially involving you as the academic, beyond setting up the situation. Students in a group are asked to share their skills base with each other so that the best decision can be made as to which students will undertake which tasks. You can offer a list of possible skills areas, but then let the students work through the inventory in their own way and share their results in whichever way works best for the group. This could be immediate, in person at the time or in the following session, if timing allows. Sometimes students prefer to offer their inventory online by e-mail or in an online learning space dedicated to the group.

In offering the list of skills areas you could produce a checklist with tickboxes, but it usually makes more sense to offer them a series of five or six 'skills areas' on a sheet of paper or online form. In each skill area you can offer a few examples so that they get the idea and are inspired to think positively about their own skill set.

 TOP TIP

There are two interrelated purposes of a skills inventory. The ostensible aim is to ensure that the tasks within a group are allocated to best effect. The less obvious (but also important) function is to ensure that members of a group gel together well, with everyone being given the chance to be involved. For this reason, design your skills inventory so that the widest possible set of skills can be captured.

 CHECKLIST

The skills inventories your students produce will be particular to your group, but you might include skills areas such as:

- languages
- administration
- groupworking
- acquisition of resources
- chairing
- technology
- presenting
- editing
- marketing
- technical areas
- creative areas.

Psychometric-/personality-type testing

As with learning needs analyses, you would probably not want to take the time to administer full psychometric tests, even if you were in a position to do so. There is also some debate around the relevance and value of the findings of some of these tests and that is a theoretical morass into which you would not want to venture. However, there are some fairly simple tests to be found that produce general indicators as to teamwork and the ways in which individuals work best within a team.

You might like to ask your students if they have ever undertaken such tests and whether or not they would like to volunteer for particular tasks in a group as the result of their findings or else spend a little of your time giving them the chance to take the tests at the beginning of a series of dynamic learning events. As with skills inventories, we would see these also as group bonding exercises.

 WORD OF WARNING

If you set up a skills inventory or group analysis opportunity, you are implying that you and all group members will respond to this information. This is sometimes just not possible, so make it clear to the group before you enter these waters that they are only one or two of the many factors that will shape the activities to come.

Recording events

Opinion is sharply divided over the educational benefits of filming or making audio records of dynamic learning events. Presentation skills, for example, are sometimes taught by repeatedly filming students giving presentations and then watching those recordings with them in a supportive environment, offering tips for improvement. Some educators, however, feel that this is a counterproductive approach and would never film students as they helped them improve their presentation skills.

To some extent, this need not be your decision, but you do have a responsibility. You need to be particularly clear about issues of confidentiality, expectations about who will have access to the recordings and, indeed, who owns them. If the members of a group feel that filming or recording sounds will be useful, perhaps to lodge it online or maybe so that they can reflect on their skills development or record the method and result of an experiment, they will voice this opinion. The chances are that you will agree with their view, but make sure that each member of the group really is happy with this plan and be sure to point out any potential barriers to learning that this might throw up.

 CHECKLIST

If you are considering either allowing or encouraging an audio recording or filming of students in a dynamic learning environment, you might like to consider the following questions with them before they go ahead.

- Are all members of the group involved in the decision?
- Why do they want to record or film?
- How will the material be used to aid learning?
- Have they all been filmed or had their voices recorded before? Are they all aware of how they look on film or sound on an audiofile?
- Are they aiming to lodge the material in a public online space?
- How long will the material stay there? Are they able to remove it later?
- If the material is to be lodged on a virtual learning environment, who will have access?
- Does the institution have permission to use the material elsewhere (for example, for publicity purposes)?
- Do consent forms have to be signed?
- Does the ethics committee have to be consulted?

This may seem like a daunting list, but it is worth getting it right before anyone commits to a process that can have such important effects on the learning process.

Peer support and assessment

A dynamic learning environment lends itself to continuous informal peer support and assessment: this is part of its appeal. In general terms, your role could be likened to hosting a good party – mingling as necessary, making sure that groups are working well together, keeping conversations on track and so forth. Much of the learning is being controlled by the students, who are supporting each other in their new discoveries.

However, there are situations when more formal peer review might be encouraged or endorsed by you. This might involve, for example, one group of students interrogating the experimental lab results of another group, peer assessment of an online resource created by students, or comments on presentation performances. This can be a highly productive experience, as long as you set the parameters.

Students are often not used to being involved in peer review so can tend either to avoid any incisive criticism of their peers at all or else couch it in such terms that it comes across as crass and negative when it was intended to be helpful. There are several ways in which the convenor of the dynamic learning environment can counteract this tendency.

- Create your own exemplar of work for viewing (a sample wiki page or handout or film) and ask students to criticise it. As they do, guide them towards the most productive ways to do this.
- Set out 'ground rules' for feedback, such as words that should or should not be used.
- Ask them to review the feedback that they have already given. Is it helpful? Is it clear?
- Explain that all feedback must lead to the opportunity for change. Vague comments with no clear sense of a path for improvement should be avoided, as should criticism about an aspect of a presentation – such as a foreign accent – that cannot be changed readily.
- Set a time limit for feedback. Students need to know that there is an end-point for the project.
- Decide in advance whether or not you are going to be the final arbiter of the product of their learning – will yours be the ultimate 'critical voice'?

As we look back, we can see at a glance that this chapter is littered with checklists, additional advice and words of warning. This accurately reflects the complexity of a dynamic learning environment. It is not for the faint-hearted educator as it demands high levels of engagement, commitment and teaching skill. Having said that, it is also hugely rewarding. You can witness learning in action to the point where you can see your students' skills and confidence growing right in front of you. It is an exciting environment for an educator and one that we would encourage you to try.

Six

LECTURES

We are going to approach this area of your teaching life by structuring a chapter around preparing for and delivering your first lecture. We are aware that you may have given several (or perhaps, very many) lectures already, but we think it is useful to take you back to the beginning, helping you to make sure that you have considered with us every facet of this learning event. It also allows you to use the chapter in the way that fits your situation best. If you are very happy with one aspect of lecturing, you can skip that section here (although, being academics and so naturally curious, we suspect that you will at least skim every section).

For most lecturers, their first experience of giving a lecture remains vivid in their minds for many years. For one of us, it has remained with her even more than one might expect. She well recalls the moment when she stepped up onto a lecture stage to face her first large group of expectant students. She was much more nervous than she had expected, but, luckily, she had chosen to prepare thorough notes, almost amounting to a full script, so she could keep going regardless of anything, which was just as well. Ten minutes from the end, just when she began to think she had given a creditable performance, a student stood up, shouted 'Fishcakes!' at the top of his voice and staggered from the room.

She knew that some students drink beer in the daytime, she had even heard of students turning up to lectures drunk, but this experience, in her inaugural lecture, means that every aspect of the event, from conception through preparation to delivery, is etched indelibly on her memory. You will be pleased to know that she kept going despite the student, then heaved a huge sigh of relief when it was all over.

Why give a lecture?

We can almost hear you answering that question without needing a moment's thought. The answer for many would be, 'Because I have to'. This may be true and, for many academics, giving lectures is, if not exactly unpleasant, still an experience for which they would not rush to volunteer. Many academics, but not by any means all. For some, it is an entirely positive experience; they relish the chance to share their knowledge and love the sense of theatre that can be involved in giving a lecture.

Most of us probably take a view somewhere around the midpoint between these two extremes – seeing lectures as a challenge, but one that we are happy enough to include in our day-to-day professional lives, something we know can, at times, be thrilling. However, this more positive viewpoint comes with experience, so, for now, you might be more inspired by considering how lecturing can contribute to your life as a researcher and vice a versa.

TEACHING AND YOUR RESEARCH

Presenting a lecture is the nearest equivalent to giving a paper or presentation about your research at a conference, so every lecture to your students is an opportunity to develop your skills related to an important research dissemination technique. All of the advice and suggestions we provide below about preparing for a lecture might well be included in a chapter on giving conference presentations. In both cases you need to consider issues such as what is expected of the presentation by those who asked you to do it and the audience receiving it (not always an exact match!), what level of understanding of the topic the audience already has and how it can be helped to know and understand more, what the context of the presentation is and how it might influence what and how you say things, how you can prepare to fit the time allowed and how you can deal effectively with the inevitable nerves.

One thing is certain. Learning to plan and execute a clear, concise, audible lecture that the students benefit from will be a good rehearsal for dealing with the more demanding audience at a conference. If you have given a conference presentation before embarking on your lecturing career, then you will have some skills already and you should find the audience for your first lecture much less demanding, much more willing to accept that you have expertise it lacks. Either way, the two experiences are mutually supportive

Having thought with you for a moment about some of the reasons for us all giving lectures, we will now take you through the process stage by stage.

Getting the brief

If you are devising your own module, you will be the one to decide the topic area for lectures, but it is just as likely that someone else will be asking you to lecture on their module. This may be a module you already know to some extent because you lead seminars on the module or perhaps a module you know hardly at all, but which has one lecture slot that obviously fits your expertise. This is perhaps an ideal situation, but be ready for the fact that you might be asked to give a lecture on a topic about which you are far less expert than you would like to be. This happens to us all from time to time and is most productively viewed as a stimulating challenge rather than a disaster waiting to happen on the grounds that your approach can lead to a self-fulfilling prophecy!

If the area in which you are being asked to lecture is not one that you feel very confident about, think for a moment before you refuse. The first point to consider is, just how much can these students know? If, for example, it is a general lecture to a group of undergraduates in their first year at university, your general grounding in the subject, perhaps supplemented with a little extra research, will be all that you need. After all, how much did you know about your subject at that stage in your academic career? Indeed, we would suggest that if you feel you know too little to give the lecture, you are probably in an ideal position to give it.

The commonest problem for less experienced lecturers is that they try to cram into a lecture every single thing they possibly can and then cannot see how they can reduce it at all. It is actually far easier to work up to the right lecture length as you gather material than work down from an initial draft that would have a run time of three hours. By the way, for the purposes of this chapter we will be working on the basis of hour-long lectures, even though we are aware that they can be of different lengths. If you are going to be giving a lecture of much more than that, it makes sense to use this chapter to plan it so you can give students a break in the middle, effectively giving two (or more) lectures in one lecture slot.

The casual approach

You might assume that a lecture request would come in the form of an e-mail or it might be pointed out to you that the teaching timetable you have been given includes some lectures. In fact, you might well be asked to give a lecture in passing, in a corridor, as you are going off to do something else. Beware of this type of request. It may be the legitimate action of a colleague who knows you would be the perfect person for a particular lecture, but it might be a colleague trying to offload a difficult or unpopular lecture on to the first enthusiastic-looking person who comes into view. As you cannot easily decide which it is on the spot, always ask to have the details of the lecture sent to you by e-mail before you commit. You might like the challenge of the lecture, but you need to be clear about what you are taking on.

Being clear

If you are asked to give a lecture, you obviously have the right to know what is involved. Despite what you may be thinking, lectures do not have to be trials of strength, with you having to guess what is required of you and hope that you get it right rather than risk looking foolish by not knowing. As you work through this chapter and ask yourself the questions we raise, if you are uncertain, then ask for the information you need. If you are still unsure, then ask someone else. You will not want to face a lecture distracted by doubts about what you are doing.

Regular or new lecture?

One of the first questions we would urge you to ask is whether or not this is a brand new lecture. If it is, then you will have a relatively free hand with it; if it is to be a regular lecture and you are taking it over from a colleague, the guidance you are given might be much more specific and narrow. If you are asked to provide a straight replacement, then it will be clear how it fits into the series and what forward and backward references can be made to material in other lectures.

Communicate by planning

If you are starting to feel awkward asking lots of questions about a lecture brief or you are being given conflicting advice, try producing a relatively detailed plan of the lecture and sharing this as a draft for discussion with whoever asked you to give the lecture. This provides an easy way for you to agree on the scope. Spider diagrams work well in this setting as they have a fluidity about them that makes it feel easy to delete or add sections to the proposed content.

Using plans can also help you to work through ideas for a series of lectures on a module or course that you are running/convening. It can be difficult to remember the detail of every lecture in a series, but if instead you plan each lecture and then compare plans it is far easier to see how they fit together. Also, you ensure minimal overlap and maximum coverage when you compare them in this outline form.

WORD OF WARNING

There may be times when you are asked to give a lecture that is a regular part of a series and, in trying to help you, the organiser might suggest that all you have to do is read aloud someone else's lecture notes. If there is a last-minute panic because someone has been taken ill, this might be unavoidable, but, generally speaking, we would urge against this approach. It seems like a gift, but most lecturers would find it hard to give a convincing lecture from someone else's notes. Even if it is a regular lecture and you are constrained as to what you can include in it, you will probably find the experience far more productive (as will your students) if you are speaking your own words rather than effectively ventriloquising for an absent colleague. You could use the notes provided to extract the key points to be made, then construct your own version of the story.

Thinking in context

A lecture is intended to be a personal expression of your knowledge, gleaned from your learning and research, tempered by the requirements of the course or module for which it is being given. It is positively beneficial for you to follow your own style of delivery and engage with your audience in the way that suits you best. We have all enjoyed the experience of great lectures that remain with us still and, if you think back to the ones you have enjoyed most, they were probably delivered in a variety of styles.

So, individuality is good, but isolation is not. Students are, for the most part, a conservative bunch. They like to know what to expect and then be given it. They do not like to be bored, but they can find change uncongenial, particularly if you look slightly uncomfortable while you are delivering the lecture. We would not, of course, suggest that you give a bland lecture just so as to avoid any possibility of startling the students, but you might want to attend a lecture or two in the series yourself, as well as talking to colleagues about what they are planning to do. This will allow you to adjust your style to the general culture or ambience of the lecture series without entirely reneging on your own most comfortable approach.

Lecture performance

Academics often refer to how well they performed in a lecture and, in many ways, it is a performance, but there are differences between the types of performance that the students will expect, often depending on their discipline area. Some lectures are just that – reading aloud from a prepared script with no deviation. Some lecturers try to add variety with the occasional ad lib section, but will still essentially stick to a script. A few – a very few – will give an apparently spontaneous lecture with no notes at all. For most of those we asked about this, they said that, actually, they have simply memorised a whole script and then have the talent to make it *look* spontaneous.

Some lectures are not so much lectures as presentations, with a full data projector slide show and a lecturer who is using this to prompt the performance. Sometimes a lecturer may, instead, take a very casual approach, simply standing and apparently rambling (in an inspiring and informative way, of course), if he or she has experience of presenting and is speaking about a topic well within his or her field of expertise.

We would never assume that any particular method is inherently better than any other. In fact, it would be impossible even to say that one method is livelier than another or more interactive – they all have challenges and opportunities. Perhaps the best place to start is to think about the types of lectures you received during your own undergraduate years. This is probably the surest guide, but you could supplement it by asking colleagues how they tend to lecture.

Teaching aids

It is a good idea to check what is 'usual' for the students you are about to lecture. Of course, you will be guided principally by your judgement as to what teaching aids would best support the learning experience you are trying to create. Beyond this, you might think strategically. If students are not used to *any* teaching aids being used, something more advanced used with a 'light touch' could perk them up – an image shown through a data projector, perhaps, or a handout that is interactive. Conversely, if the student group is used to a full slide show for every lecture, the simplicity of a lecturer just making eye contact and talking to them could be very appealing.

Interactivity

To a great degree, you will be in control of the level of interactivity. If you would like your student group to respond to questions or make comments during the lecture, you can encourage this, which you might do if you are hoping to develop an inquisitive, interactive way of tackling a topic. If, on the other hand, you have a plethora of facts that simply need to be conveyed with energy and confidence but without interruptions, then this is the kind of learning environment you will encourage.

What is the right level will depend on what you deem useful, but check first what the group is used to. If lecturers on the course regularly leave ten minutes at the end of the event for questions and answers, discouraging interruptions during, you would at least want to know that this is the norm and only break from it if you have good reason to do so. If you do want to do so, then it would be sensible to alert the students to your breaking with tradition and why it is happening.

THE VOICE OF EXPERIENCE PLUS TEACHING AND YOUR RESEARCH

We have spoken several times about the style, traditions or cultures that students are used to. Although we have worked together in both research and teaching capacities, our discipline backgrounds are quite dissimilar. This has alerted us to the varied expectations of undergraduate students in different disciplines and has also helped us to understand better the different styles of presentation that our postgraduate students will need to master when disseminating their research to discipline-specific audiences. One set of disciplines would traditionally expect a conference paper to be read out from a detailed script whereas another would find that unusual, preferring a presentation delivered by more spontaneous elaboration on main points presented using some form of slide. You will by now know which is the most usual form of presentation expected in your discipline culture, having 'grown up' in it.

Learning hurdles

The particular educational needs of each member of your student group must be taken into account from the earliest preparations. This might, for example, affect the layout or font size of your handouts and other visual materials or sway decisions about including any group activity during a lecture.

These needs tend to have less of a direct impact on a lecture than on a seminar, but be ready for notetakers sitting beside students, audio recording equipment placed beside you and students who seem to be doing nothing because they have a notetaker or are recording what you are saying.

Timing the preparation

There are academics who thoroughly enjoy rushing around the day before a lecture telling anybody who will listen that they have an important lecture to give in less than 24 hours and the whole situation is very stressful. Their colleagues will usually smile sympathetically, recognising that this is how the lecturer has chosen to work and the bluster is a way of preparing for the challenge of the lecture.

There are others who never mention their lectures. They prepare well in advance, leave themselves plenty of time to rehearse, are in control of their time and material and simply get on with the task ahead of them. This latter approach sounds the more professional of the two – it is somehow deemed more admirable to have thought through the issues in advance and made no fuss – but, in reality, neither approach seems to result in a better or worse lecture.

The secret is twofold. First, be who you are. If you love a bit of a flurry to keep your adrenalin levels up, then you are likely to be a last-minute lecture writer. Just make sure that your approach is not allowed to irritate your colleagues. If you feel comfortable when you have more time to mull it over, take more time over it. Second, leave plenty of time to rehearse, whichever way you approach the writing.

We have been lecturing for many years, yet we would still never give a lecture without rehearsing it first, to time. This might involve no more than reading our script or notes through aloud (or at least muttered under our breath). This is not about stage fright but, rather, ensuring that we have the tone and quality of the lecture right. When you are preparing your first few lectures, leave yourself as long to rehearse as to prepare and write. That way you can leave it alone to settle between rehearsals and ensure you are confident on the day.

 TOP TIP

The very idea of your lecture is likely to hang over you a little in the days before you have to deliver it. If you expect to get very nervous, you might prepare it well in advance so that preparations and nerves will not distract you too much from your research as the lecture approaches. On the other hand, guard against insouciance – an adrenalin-free performance tends to lack passion and heart!

Decisions to make

It makes sense to glean as much information as you can about a lecture situation before you begin to prepare. The circumstances will not necessarily make a huge difference to what happens, but they could affect some aspects of your lecture planning and delivery.

Number of students

The number of students expected at the lecture might not change your delivery style, but it might change the structure. If you were thinking of taking ten minutes during the lecture for students to talk in pairs and feed back some ideas, you might hesitate if there are 320 students.

We remember hoping desperately for the smallest possible number of students for our first few lectures, believing somehow that to lecture to 40 students was 'almost like a seminar' and so not too daunting. In practice, the number of listeners will make little difference to your teaching experience, so try not to be put off by a large student group.

Level of knowledge

This might come as a natural, almost subconscious, element in your planning if you know the module well and lead one of its seminars. If this is not the case, always double-check with someone who is experienced (both in lecturing and on the module or course in question). You may be surprised at just how basic you are expected to be. It would not be unusual, for example, to recap material from the previous year at the beginning of a lecture or assume that students have not read all of the relevant material in advance.

 WORD OF WARNING

Try not to get cross about how little students know in advance of a learning event. Sometimes they claim to know virtually nothing at all just so as to avoid the pressure of being asked to elaborate on what they do know. There is no point in rather challengingly ploughing through a lecture assuming prior knowledge of material to a cloud of blank faces. Five minutes spent at the outset covering basic points and explaining how the material fits into the module will result in grateful faces and a far more positive teaching and learning experience.

Do they know you? Do they know each other?

A lecture is not a social event in the way that a seminar is, but it is nevertheless useful to know if this is a meeting of relative strangers or a well-knit group of fellow academic travellers. It need not create a hurdle either way, but it might subtly alter the atmosphere of the occasion and it is worth knowing in advance.

TOP TIP

Try not to judge your lecture success by how readily a group of students responds to your questions or invitation to speak up. There are too many variables to assume that a quiet group is somehow 'your fault' and the learning experience might be no less valuable or productive just because the students do not feel like talking today. Remember that they have a perfect right to sit back and wait to be entertained and informed – a lecture is a little like the theatre in that way. Be ready for the possibility that they might not feel like talking and adapt your material in response to this; becoming disgruntled and agitated will not improve the situation.

What time of day is the lecture?

Again, this might not have much effect on your lecture experience, but a 9 a.m. lecture is more likely to mean that you will have some bleary-eyed latecomers than would be the case with a lecture later in the day. Equally, if you are giving a lecture straight after lunch or at the end of the learning day, try to add some visual or interactive elements if you can and try not to take offence if some members of your audience become sleepy during the lecture.

Show you care

A colleague of ours has a set of four elegant designer dresses. She wears them to give lectures. The rest of the time she happily wears jeans, but, for lectures, she dresses up. We have noticed this and we know that the students have, too. The effect on students is that they know she is taking the lecture seriously, she cares about the occasion and, by extension, about the students and their learning needs.

We are not suggesting here (sadly) that we should all be provided with designer outfits in order to lecture, but we are making the point that students appreciate good-quality contact time and have a right to receive it. Scrappy handouts in the form of poor-quality photocopies from elderly books, with no explanatory notes, are not going to inspire them. Simply reading though a draft book chapter that has little relevance to their module syllabus will not impress them either (although this can work well for postgraduate seminars). So, when you are standing up in front of a large group of students, preparing to spend an hour of your life (and theirs) teaching them, you will want to elicit the best possible response and showing that you see their needs as important is the best way to achieve this.

Preparing to write the lecture

It should perhaps go without saying that your lecture will need to fit with the learning aims and objectives of the module within which it sits. It will also need to add to the body of knowledge being offered on the module, so it is worth checking the full module description before you begin. Leading seminars on a module might make you think that you know the module well, but it is worth double-checking at this stage. Beyond this, there are several more aspects to consider.

Is it a core lecture?

A core lecture is one that conveys vital information. This might be because the lecture is at the start of the module, grounding the students in a knowledge area, or the material on which the lecture is based is going to form part of the assessment for the module. The delivery might not vary greatly from one type of lecture to the other, but you will obviously want to ensure that every scrap of necessary information is given out if this is to be a core lecture and you might want to be doubly sure that this has happened by providing a data-rich handout.

 EXERCISE 13

A core lecture will necessarily focus on just a few key areas, giving as much detail as possible. If you are not sure about how to begin to write a core lecture, attend a few. As you listen, note down the key areas that are being covered (and ignore all of the detail). This is surprisingly difficult to do when you first try it, but, once you have done it a few times, you will become adept at spotting the essential points and then you will be ready to produce the skeleton of your own core lecture.

What do your students need to get out of it?

The obvious answer – information – is actually the least likely to be correct. They can find information in books and journals or turn to the Internet. So, what makes a lecture different from these sources? It is the range of learning opportunities it offers. In a lecture, students can:

- be inspired by your enthusiasm
- ask you questions
- find reassurance in your comments
- see how you approach a subject area

- see the results of your research in action
- gain access to your unpublished material
- feel part of a space for learning.

That is what makes for a good lecture – it is why it feels like a significant moment in the students' day, however many lectures they have attended.

 WORD OF WARNING

We have just been asking you to focus, rightly, on the needs of your students. However nervous you are, and however keen to impress and make your mark with your students and your peers, a lecture is never about you and how you would like to be seen – it is always about the students. Resist the temptation for intellectual showmanship at the expense of supporting your students in the way that they need most.

THE VOICE OF EXPERIENCE

From our own student days we can each remember being bemused and demotivated by the occasional lecturers who seemed to speak in a language far divorced from ours in terms of vocabulary and those who seemed to put themselves on a pedestal above the mere mortals who were students. One of our colleagues, recalling his student days, put it thus:

'As I became more experienced, I, and my fellow students, began to recognise that the apparent showing off of erudition was actually a protective barrier for the lecturer to hide behind to ward off potential questions and challenges. Sadly, once this was realised, we lost respect for him – the very opposite of what he intended, I'm sure.'

You cannot do too much

One of the unexpected things about lectures for those not used to giving them is just how little you can say in them. You cannot expect to cover more than six main points. This is not about timing; it is about how humans work. You would have time in an hour to cover a multitude of areas, but your students would not be able to remember what you said, your lecture would lose focus and impact and you would muddle yourself and your students. Six points is a guide, not a rule, so four or five main points would also be fine, but trying to cover eight or nine areas would feel too crowded. We will talk more in the next section about the structure and content of your lecture, but bear the 'six-point rule' in mind throughout.

General or niche?

We have already talked about whether or not your lecture is to be a core lecture, but you have another, similar decision to make. Are you aiming to give a general lecture, to help the students gain the amount of knowledge they need to position themselves confidently in a subject area, or are you going to deliver a niche lecture, with more specialised content or a particular (perhaps controversial) point of view?

The choice you make here will depend on several factors and will be rooted in the needs of your group of students at this stage on their course. Either type of lecture can be enjoyable to prepare and satisfying to give, but you need to decide initially which way you are going. You also need to make it clear to the *students* which type of lecture you are about to give them, so that they do not receive a niche lecture and assume you have given them the last word on an area when what you were trying to do was spark interest and provoke debate.

Planning the lecture

The structure of most lectures is fairly standard, regardless of content. It should include the following steps.

1   A check that all of the students (and so you, too) are in the right place for the right lecture.

 TOP TIP

This is a good moment to see if you can spot any students you are teaching in a seminar group and smile at them in recognition. It makes them feel special and you more confident.

2   An introduction to you (even if you think they probably all know you), giving them your office location or e-mail address so that they can contact you after the lecture if they have queries.

 TOP TIP

If you are feeling nervous, writing up your contact details on the board gives you a chance to turn away from the audience for a few moments so as to compose yourself.

3 A recap of what has happened in the module so far.

4 A general introduction to the material you aim to cover and how this fits into the learning for the module.

5 A guide to the way in which you plan to approach the material (that is, whether the lecture represents a general approach or a niche aspect of the topic).

6 The specific areas you aim to cover.

 WORD OF WARNING

Students become anxious if you tell them the outline of the lecture and they miss it – they like to know where they are going as the lecture progresses – so, if you can, make sure that this information is written down on the handout or is shown on a slide.

7 Reassurance about their access to the material you are about to use (if they are to be given a handout at the end, for example, or if the material they are about the see will be lodged on a VLE).

8 The main body of the lecture (which we will discuss below).

9 A strong conclusion.

 TOP TIP

It is best to avoid phrases such as 'in conclusion' or 'one final point' towards the end of the lecture, as some students will take this as their cue to rustle about and start packing up their things, which is extremely off-putting.

10 Questions and answers, if this is the usual structure of a lecture in your department.

 WORD OF WARNING

Although students may have smiled enthusiastically during the lecture, this is no guarantee that they will ask questions in front of the entire group and it can leave a flat feeling to a lecture if you ask for questions and get silence. Unless we are specifically asked to include a question and answer session, we prefer to finish a few minutes ahead of time and tell the students that we will stay in the room for a while in case any of them have questions.

The main body of the lecture will, of course, be up to you. Remember that you might not want to start writing the lecture straight away – it could be a better idea (particularly if you have any doubts about the brief or how the lecture will fit into a series) to make a rough plan at this stage. That way you can leave it alone for a while so when you come back to it you can see any glaring omissions. You can also use it to share your ideas for the lecture with colleagues.

 CHECKLIST

In any lecture there are balances to create and so choices to make between:

- giving information and throwing out ideas/questions to inspire their thinking
- reassuring them about facts and challenging them about approaches/theories that might be contradictory
- scripted talking and improvisation
- talking to them and asking for questions
- talking and taking time to offer visual materials.

Although some of this might come instinctively, it is still a good idea to work through this checklist as you prepare your lecture to make sure that you are happy with the way it is structured.

Writing the lecture

How long should it take to write it?

If you feel familiar with the material and certain of your approach, a lecture might take just a few hours to write. If, though, rather than being a 'fast and furious' writer you are a 'slow but steady' scholar, you might come back to it again and again over several days. Neither way is better than the other, although you will want to make sure that taking your time is a productive approach rather than feel it is just a task hanging over you as a distraction for weeks.

Our main advice would be to stand firm and choose the way you know you tend to work best. By all means ask colleagues how long they take to write their lectures, but remember that there is no one right way to do it – and people do like to embellish a little from time to time!

How long should the word count be?

This is an unanswerable question in some ways. One of us has just looked back over her last three lecture scripts and they were all around

4000 to 5000 words for hour-long lectures. She would usually include four or five occasions when she would improvise and move away from the script, just to keep it feeling more like natural speech and maintain the students' interest. Of course, this is no more than an example of how one lecturer prepares, but you might find it handy to have as a guideline.

How should it look?

We seem to be assuming above that you will be standing up and giving a lecture with a script but, of course, this may not be the case at all. You could be giving a presentation with full technology to help you along or you may prefer to work from prompt cards if you are not going to improvise throughout (which would be a high-risk strategy unless you were sure you could cope with this approach). You might combine approaches by working from a script but showing visual materials as well.

THE VOICE OF EXPERIENCE

If you are planning to use notes of any kind, you might consider a few of these practical points collated from our colleagues' and our own experience.

- Normal A4 size paper has a tendency to transmit and exaggerate any tremor of your hands – choose thin card or A5 sheets to reduce the possibility of your nerves showing.
- Pages have a wicked tendency to get themselves out of order – remember to number them and consider using a treasury tag in the corner to allow you to fold them back as you move through the pages, preventing them from decorating the floor as you do so.
- If you are using slides as prompts, then make sure that you know how to advance the slides before the students come into the room.

Knowing the space

Although from time to time we all lecture in rooms or lecture theatres with which we are unfamiliar, it is a good idea – at least for your first few lectures – to check out the space in advance.

CHECKLIST

As you look around the space in which you will be lecturing, ask yourself questions such as these.

- Do you know the space from previous events? Do the students?
- Is it big enough? Too big?
- Is there technology if you need it? Do you have the technician's number in case of breakdowns?
- Are you familiar with the technology in this particular space?
- Is there a board or flipchart? Pens?
- Do you know where everything is?
- Are there any barriers to communication, such as a poor room layout? Can you change them?
- Is there a lectern?
- Is the area in which you will be standing too cluttered? Can you change this?
- What are the light levels like?
- Are there windows that open?
- Will the seating plan work well? Can you change it or ask students to sit in a particular pattern?

If the answers to the questions in the checklist cause you to have serious concerns about the room, you might be able to book another. Usually, though, it is a case of turning up early (if you can) and altering things to make them more conducive to your teaching plans before the lecture begins.

Getting your timing right

An hour is actually 45 minutes.

Perhaps, even less. The usual protocol is to finish a lecture ten minutes before the hour's up to allow students to get to their next learning event on time. It rarely takes less than four or five minutes for students to turn up after it was due to start and for you to give out your contact details. That takes it down to 45 minutes and, if you have a question and answer session at the end, that will take at least 10 minutes if it is to be a useful teaching space.

Time warping

Added to the already dwindling lecture time is the issue of the strange time warps that seem to happen during lectures. You would probably assume that your lecture would actually run faster on the day than when you rehearsed it because your nerves would incline you to rush, yet, in reality, it always seems to take longer. You plan to improvise briefly on one point, but, in your adrenalin-fuelled enthusiasm, you can easily find yourself talking far longer than expected or explaining a point that seemed clear in your lecture notes but is now causing you anxiety. You might be using visual aids with a group that likes to take a long time to study them – far longer than you had allowed for in your rehearsal.

All of these things can conspire to throw out your timing. Usually this makes your planned timing too cramped, although, occasionally, it can work the other way and you have time to spare. If the lecture finishes five minutes early, nobody is likely to complain and, if you put some 'ad lib' markers to yourself towards the end of a lecture, denoting aspects of the topic on which you could elaborate if you had to, you might be able to stretch it so as to finish near to time.

Always rehearse to under time

Given that the commonest problem is a lecture running for longer than expected, it makes sense to rehearse it to a little under time. For an hour's lecture, we would assume that it will actually be 45 minutes' speaking time and rehearse to around 42 minutes, with 'ad lib' markers so we could stretch the material productively if necessary.

Never, ever run over time

We have mentioned before the unyielding attitude students have towards events that run over. However fascinating your material, they will switch off as soon as they judge that you should have finished talking. They simply do not care that you may have spent many hours producing the lecture: if you cannot deliver it to time, they are not interested. Worse still, they will see you as unprofessional and willing to steal their time from them.

This potential problem is not easily tackled right at the end of the lecture as they may spot it if you rather abruptly end the material by just trying to cut yourself off. Instead, check the clock about 25–30 minutes into the event and make sure that you are at the right point for the time. If you include some flexibility within your lecture notes you can make any adjustments easily enough. This flexibility comes most usually either by having a series of 'ad lib' points throughout the lecture, which can be omitted as needed, or a whole section of the lecture that you do not introduce at the outset of the event so that you can omit it entirely if things are not going to plan.

TOP TIP

Some lecturers find it useful to include a timing reminder within their notes, either by writing 'halfway' at the appropriate point or, if they fear that this might distract them, by striking a highlighter line through one page to show that this is roughly the halfway point.

If you know you tend to get nervous, you could add other kinds of reminders, ideally in a different-coloured font. These might include to give out your name at the beginning or show a slide or smile and make eye contact with the students from time to time.

THE VOICE OF EXPERIENCE

Earlier we suggested that students appreciate having a note at the beginning of a session, an advance organiser, setting out what you intend to cover. Many of our experienced colleagues said that they, too, like to have a note of what they intend to cover so they can check on their progress during the lecture. One colleague saw the 'advance organiser' handout for students as a compromise, or a bridge, between the full text and the prompt card method.

Practising

How much you want to rehearse your lecture will depend largely on your general approach to speaking in public. If you have spoken at a conference or given a seminar paper, you could follow the same rehearsal schedule you used for that event. If you feel reasonably confident about speaking in public, you might want to do little more than give a mock lecture in your own home to a blank wall, just to see how the material fits together.

 CHECKLIST

If you know you would be better (in terms of nerves and performance) for having several rehearsals, try to build progression into your practice schedule.

1 Rehearse for the first time simply to see if the material roughly fits the time, remembering to leave some space for referring to any teaching aids you are using and for any improvised sections you are intending to include.

(Continued)

(Continued)

2 If you need to make alterations to the material to improve the timing, move now to your final prompting method. That is, revise your script or move to prompt cards or make sure that your visual aids will offer you enough support.

3 Rehearse again with the revised material to ensure that it now fits the time you have available. For this rehearsal, ask a friend or colleague to listen if you want to make sure you have not left any gaps and that the material flows well as a whole.

4 If you have left space in your lecture for improvisations, practise these at this stage, along with the more scripted or formal part of the lecture. You will not want them to be over-rehearsed, but neither will you want to surprise yourself on the day with what comes out of your mouth! One rehearsal will probably be enough to reassure you that you have something to say in the 'ad lib' gaps without losing the creativity of that part of the lecture.

5 If you have not spoken in a large lecture space before, it makes sense to let your voice get a feel for the space. You might not want to practise your whole lecture in the space, but spending some time talking into the space will help to acclimatise you. Ideally, take a friend or colleague along with you for this rehearsal and ask them to sit at the back and then the far sides so as to make sure that you can be heard throughout the space.

However thoroughly you prepare and however much you rehearse, in the end you will just have to go for it and give the lecture. What a moment! You might be calmer than you had expected (some people are) or you might be riven with nerves, but you can cling to the thought that you have prepared as well as you can and it will be over almost before you know it. It is a little like a fairground ride – nerve-wracking in prospect, but then it goes by far too fast and, as soon as you get off, you want to do it all over again.

Nerves

In this situation being nervous is not only a sensible human response but also actually a good thing. There is a real sense of occasion about a lecture and this is enhanced by your nerves. It means that you will perform to your best, with a passion and adrenalin–fuelled energy that will inspire your students.

Your task is to accept that your nervousness is a good thing, but not to let it master you. You can lose out to nerves if your anxiety makes you act awkwardly or if it stops you being able to perform as you would like.

CHECKLIST

The awkwardness caused by nerves can come out in a variety of ways, so ask a friend to view your rehearsal and final performance with the checklist below, so that you can work to rid yourself of any of these kinds of problems:

- fiddling – with your hair, the keys in your pocket, your notes, your clothes
- rhythmic movement – repetitive clicking of a pen or adjustment of a pointer
- swaying from side to side
- rocking to and fro, from toe to heel and back again
- repetitive use of certain words
- moving too far forwards, invading the students' space
- forgetting to use your teaching aids fully
- turning so far towards the board or screen that you cannot turn back again easily
- hiding – either by holding up notes in front of your face or turning to face the screen too much
- staring at one or two people and not realising that you are making them uncomfortable
- forgetting to make eye contact at all
- forgetting to smile.

This takes time and practice to get right, so keep referring back to this checklist over time, until all of your awkwardness is banished. You might make your own checklist of anything else that your supporters have noticed, but try to correct just one thing at a time rather than overtaxing yourself, which can make everything worse.

Not performing quite as well as you would like due to your nerves is less noticeable to members of the audience than the problems listed above but will still have a detrimental impact on your confidence.

 CHECKLIST

As with the previous checklist, ask a friend to help you in selecting those which apply to you (some of them will only be obvious to you):

- Blushing
- Stammering
- Speaking too fast
- Running out of breath
- Losing the sense of the words, leading to strange breaks in sentences
- Speaking in a monotone, with no real variety in your voice.

Again, these problems will take time to fix, but working through breathing and relaxation techniques can help hugely.

One note of reassurance: although these checklists are enough to make anyone shy away from ever giving a lecture, you can gain reassurance from the fact that most of them are irrelevant to your students, who will not even notice them. Your performance, and your pleasure in the occasion, will improve as you work on these issues, but you will have given good lectures regardless of anxiety-related glitches.

THE VOICE OF EXPERIENCE

We have mentioned before that adrenalin is produced when we are nervous or afraid – it is intended to help you fight or take flight. Since we are assuming that you are not going to resort to the latter reaction, then you could do well to reduce its effects by trying some of these ruses described to us by fellow lecturers:

- burning some of it up in advance by taking a brisk walk to the lecture room
- with the door firmly closed, doing a few exercises in the privacy of your own room
- it is the same adrenalin that dries your mouth and makes your tongue grow (or so it feels) to twice its size – be ready for that with a handy bottle of water.

TEACHING AND YOUR RESEARCH

All of the suggestions we have made about reducing the effects of nerves will apply equally well to those of you who have yet to engage in the challenging experience of presenting your research in a viva or, indeed, preparing for an interview or conference presentation. We have found that, no matter how experienced (old) we get, those kinds of situations still make us nervous – and the adrenalin still flows – but we have learnt to employ all the tricks of the trade we have described to manage and disguise the outward signs.

Some of the problems we have considered with you here tend to disappear with time, and accepting that can stop them becoming a hurdle to your being able to move forward and give a confident performance. One of us has a dreadful tendency to blush. Nothing seemed to stop it and she realised early on she was going to have to accept that this was just a part of her nature. She kept on lecturing regardless and developed a strategy whereby, when she blushed, she acknowledged it to herself and reminded herself that it would pass in time. To her amazement, one day it just stopped happening in lectures. She still blushes on all sorts of other occasions, but being able to lecture through her blushes gave her the confidence to do all sorts of other things.

Reflections

Giving a lecture for the first few times is a little like taking an exam, in that you come away from the experience with no clear sense of exactly how it went. It is only later that you can reflect, perhaps with a friend or colleague who was at the event. As with an exam, there is little point in a minutely detailed post mortem, but if you challenge yourself to take away no more than one or two points for improvement from each of those first few lectures, you will rapidly build in confidence and ability.

If you feel it would help, you could film or record your lecture so that you could play it back or listen to it and spot areas for improvement, but only do this after you have given it serious consideration. There is a natural human tendency to see only the areas for improvement and be blind to what you did well. We have been lecturing for decades and we would still rather not see ourselves on film – not because we fear we do it badly, but because we know we would bring a skewed perception to what we would see.

Giving your first lecture is a momentous event in your life as an academic. It marks your transition from a private researcher to a public purveyor of information and inspiration. As we think back to our first lectures, and look forward to think about yours, we are reminded of the words of Samuel Beckett in *Worstward Ho* (1983):

Ever tried. Ever failed. No matter. Try Again. Fail again. Fail better.

These words are on a poster outside one of the lecture theatres in which we have both taught from time to time. We think they were put there to inspire students to read or watch Beckett's work. For us, they are a reminder not that we are failures, but, rather, that no lecture can ever be 'the perfect lecture', but, every single time we do it, we are getting better (and braver).

Seven

PRODUCTIVE TEACHING AIDS

You may have heard this said many times, but it is true: *you* are your best teaching aid.

Nowadays we are faced with a plethora of potential teaching aids, including data projectors, online demonstrations, Skype and smartboards. These have been added to, rather than replacing, the older teaching aids, such as overhead projectors, flipcharts, whiteboards and blackboards. All this means that a huge number of decisions need to be made when it comes to even the simplest teaching situation.

Assume with us, for a moment, that we have developed a sudden urge to demonstrate to a group of students the joys of eating a chocolate bar. In today's teaching setting we would need to know the answers to the following questions.

- Does the teaching room have technology – if so, what types of technology?
- Do we have time to set the technology up before we teach?
- Can we make a sensible back-up plan in case it fails?
- Are we comfortable with the technology available?

Then we might have to decide which of the following options to go for:

- use an online resource to show someone else's demonstration
- film our own demonstration and show it via a data projector or online
- use a data projector to create a diagram of the process, with other slides to show the information around the topic
- use an overhead projector (OHP) to show photographs of the process
- use an online polling system to ask students to text in their views on the process
- create a wiki to allow for an interactive group response to the process

- use a smartboard to allow students to write across our pre-prepared notes
- access a virtual learning environment (VLE) to demonstrate the process.

… and so on, and so on.

The decision we finally make might be based on the following factors.

- How familiar the student group is with technology – would it inspire and excite them, bore them or distract their attention?
- How important is the demonstration? How much time do we want to devote to preparing and using a teaching aid?
- Is the demonstration a springboard to further activities or does it stand alone?
- Do we want this to be an ephemeral 'learning moment' or do we need the students to have some material to take away from the event? Does this material need to be in the form of a hard copy?

Having so many options can mean there is a tendency to spend, as you can see here, quite a large amount of teaching preparation time considering which is the best option for any one situation. This is, in general, a good thing. It inspires us to see our teaching afresh and keep alive the enthusiasm for learning among our students. However, it also allows us to become so immersed in technology (even 'old' technology) that we lose our way or rely on it too heavily.

Of course, the tendency to hide behind technology has always been with us. We remember lessons in our youth when 'teaching' was often more a case of 'writing' as teachers entered the classroom and simply wrote notes, in chalk, on a blackboard. As learners, we assiduously wrote down the notes. Much of the learning would happen later, when we reviewed the notes in our revision time. So entrenched was this means of teaching that those pupils whose eyes wandered to the window would be exhorted to 'face the board'. The assumption was that the seat of teaching in the room was the blackboard and the notes on it, rather than the person who was ostensibly 'the teacher'.

Education may have come a long way since then, but the temptation to hide is still there – it is just a more creative temptation now. It is possible – and we have seen it – for a lecturer to enter the lecture theatre with a beautifully prepared set of slides that are shown using a data projector, the lecturer effectively joining with the students in admiring the slides and never once looking away from the screen, even when talking about the slides. Some learning has happened in that space, but far less than might potentially have happened.

As we have been writing this and talking through the various visual aids we have used and enjoyed (and sometimes not enjoyed at all) we have, as was inevitable, eaten the chocolate bars that were the basis of this discussion. They were, we both agree, delicious. We wish you could have been here to share them with us and to view our gleeful delight as we bit into them, the satisfaction on our faces once they were consumed and the disappointment in our eyes now that they are gone. That is the point: in this case, just eating them would have been enough to show you all that you needed to know about the joys of eating chocolate.

 TOP TIP

Usually, simplest and most direct is best. Your standard position with regard to teaching aids should be to use only the minimum you need to achieve the desired effect.

Do you need teaching aids?

The previous section might leave you thinking that we are not keen at all on the idea of teaching aids, but this is not the case. The most appropriate teaching aid used in the right circumstances can bring your teaching to life and make an exciting and motivating learning environment.

THE VOICE OF EXPERIENCE

This is a point at which you should most definitely reflect on your own learning experiences, recalling both those occasions when you felt really engaged with learning and those that left you either bored or flummoxed. Consider what made the difference between the two. In the first case, you may have had the privilege of hearing a charismatic speaker, but, more often than not, you will have been taught by someone who took the trouble to consider the various ways in which a group of learners might connect with the material. This takes us back to our previous point about learning styles: some people learn better if they hear, others when they see, while most of us do so when we actively work with new ideas. Thus, an effective teacher uses the available media to highlight important points in a variety of ways, while at the same time remembering that it is the point which is important, not the medium.

We can think of very few occasions when you would not use any teaching aids at all. A lecture without any visual aids would come nearest, but even then you might be relying on a handout or material that has already been posted on a virtual learning environment online. The intensity of a tutorial is supported and softened by having a piece of work to discuss. Even the most casual of seminars will usually be based on some material that is under discussion and can be seen by all. A laboratory setting, however ad hoc the teaching, will allow for the visual aids in the form of demonstrations.

So, you will need teaching aids and the preparation and use of them is therefore an integral part of getting ready to teach and developing as an educator. In the next section we will analyse how you can use them to greatest effect.

 WORD OF WARNING

We are exploring here the use of 'teaching aids', not 'teachers' aids'. Never use an aid that is there simply to help you teach rather than for the benefit of the students. Of course, a slide projected onto screen is a useful prompt for you, but giving minute instructions for an activity you could easily just tell people to do always looks unprofessional, as does revealing details of timings and so on that your students do not need to know.

What options do you have?

We want to look with you at a range of teaching aids that you might have available to you and guide you in their use. We will be considering the:

- blackboard, whiteboard, flipchart
- data projector, slide projector, overhead projector
- interactive whiteboard (smartboard)
- handouts
- virtual learning environment (VLE), including 'Turnitin'
- wikis and online polling systems
- demonstration
- film and audio
- online resources and mobile phones
- students.

For each of these teaching aids we will be looking at:

- what it is/what it does
- advantages
- disadvantages
- types and amount of material to use with it
- how to use it successfully
- the ideal situation for its use.

You might use the rest of this chapter in one of two ways. You might find it helpful to read it right through, so as to get a sense of what is available, or you could use it to identify which will be the best aid for your next teaching situation and simply focus on that aid for now. Whichever way you approach it, you might want to use the checklist below to identify which aid is likely to be the easiest one for you to try out first.

 CHECKLIST

Some of the options we have listed here might be familiar to you, either because you have used them or seen others use them. Tick those teaching aids with which you are familiar — it can boost your confidence to see that this is not all new territory and will help you in targeting what you might try out next time you have an opportunity. If you have used and seen very few of them, there is no need to worry — you have an exciting time ahead!

- Blackboard, whiteboard, flipchart ☐
- Data projector, slide projector, overhead projector ☐
- Interactive whiteboard (smartboard) ☐
- Handouts ☐
- Virtual learning environment (VLE), including 'Turnitin' ☐
- Wikis and online polling systems ☐
- Demonstration ☐
- Film and audio ☐
- Online resources and mobile phones ☐
- Students. ☐

WORD OF WARNING

Teaching aids are only effective if they aid everyone in the room. *Always* check on the suitability of your teaching aids for each particular group — do any members of the group have a hearing or visual impairment or any other potential hurdle to overcome to be able to access and utilise your teaching aids fully? Consider how you might overcome such problems to everyone's advantage — using a belt and braces approach if you are not familiar with the detailed needs of your audience — and remaining flexible, having more than one idea at hand.

Blackboard, whiteboard, flipchart

What it is/what it does

A fixed or movable surface on which to write notes, either prepared before a teaching session or created during the session.

Advantages

It is always to hand if you teach in a fixed location where one is situated. You can ignore it without it being intrusive and it can be used spontaneously by you or the students.

A flipchart allows for some flexibility, in that it can be moved about, but it is heavy. Students will be very used to seeing one and so will not find it threatening. Flipchart sheets can be taken away by students, reused by you or transcribed after the event.

 TOP TIP

A flipchart can be a useful tool in group dynamics. If you turn it away from the group and write on it while the students have been left to work in groups, it is an excuse for you to break eye contact with them – in a way, you have 'left the room' and they may then be more willing to open up and talk to each other.

Disadvantages

It requires pens (of the correct type) or chalk. This might seem like a minor point, but it is a major disadvantage if you are not the only person using the board and make the assumption that pens will be available and they are not; this can lead to irritating time delays while you try to beg a pen from anyone in the vicinity of the equipment. Also, unless you take a photo of the black- or whiteboard at the end of the session, you are left with no permanent record of what was noted.

Types and amount of material to use with it

The accumulation of material on a black- or whiteboard will be natural and spontaneous in most cases. However, it will obviously not work well if you produce material that you want to refer to throughout the learning event and then find you have run out of space. If this is likely to be the case, but you want to remain 'low-tech', a flipchart is the answer, as it allows you to tear off sheets and stick them up as you go. It is for this reason that lecturers will sometimes combine the 'high-tech' data projector with the 'low-tech' flipchart.

How to use it successfully

Check your writing. Try writing up on the board and then check from the back and sides of the room that it can be read easily. Ideally ask someone else to confirm this as well.

Before you erase material or move to the next sheet of a flipchart, always ask if everyone has finished making the notes they need. Then assume that those who haven't are embarrassed and lying to you and look to see if anyone is actually still writing rather desperately.

 WORD OF WARNING

Asking the students to write on a board or flipchart requires fine judgement. While they may be happily shouting out answers for you to write on there, the physical gap between you remains. Asking them to cross that divide and take on the writing role is a big step, so ask only when you are sure that they will enjoy it.

The ideal situation for its use

A small-group teaching setting, such as a lab or seminar, when you want to create an atmosphere of sharing and creativity. Even if you are the only person actually writing on the board or flipchart, the students will be prompting the writing and this helps them – especially the visual learners – to feel part of the teaching and learning that is taking place.

THE VOICE OF EXPERIENCE

More than one of our experienced lecturers expressed the view that preparing materials needs the teacher to consider the points of view, their seats in the classroom and meaning perspective of the audience. One of them elaborated on this:

'Because writing neatly and in letters large enough and spaced well enough to be read from the back of the room can be tiresome, it is tempting to condense points to a few words. This is fine if it means expressing what you have said in a different, more concise way, but we need to be careful when summarising the contributions of others, perhaps when compiling a list of ideas from the class. It is good manners to say at the outset that you may abbreviate what is offered and then check that your précis does indeed represent what was said. I can remember as a student getting quite annoyed when a lecturer condensed my carefully phrased comments in her own words and missed the point.'

TEACHING AND YOUR RESEARCH

When your teaching includes aspects of your research, the need to express it in ways that make sense to the audience helps give you new perspectives on it, too. Using a range of media during the course of your teaching will help you to find different ways of expressing your ideas and contribute to your ability to disseminate your research to society in all its diversity, as we will demonstrate below. For instance, writing up key words to emphasise them to your audience means you have to decide what those *key* words are – a skill that will be required of you when publishing your research in journals, for instance.

Data projector, slide projector, overhead projector

What it is/what it does

Visual images are sent from a device onto a screen. A data projector uses a computer or laptop to do this, whereas a slide projector uses a carousel of physical slides and an overhead projector uses clear acetate sheets on which the images have been written by hand or printed.

Advantages

A data projector allows you to show a slick, professional set of slides.

A slide projector allows you to show slides without the hassle of transferring them to a computer; it is also relatively portable. It can seem a little old-fashioned, but then some students might enjoy this.

An overhead projector is portable, versatile, easy to use and unlikely to go wrong. It allows you and/or the students to prepare acetate sheets in the teaching setting and show them to each other quickly and easily.

Disadvantages

A data projector can fail to work, students can become bored if yours is yet another session with a data projector and it can be a distraction to have an image on the screen and a fan whirring away while you are talking through any material that is not shown via the data projector.

If a slide projector goes wrong, there is no back-up.

An overhead projector can seem old-fashioned, although students seem to get over this hurdle very quickly once it is in use. Usually reliable, but lightbulbs tend to burn out at the wrong moment, so check the equipment before you start and find the back-up bulb!

 WORD OF WARNING

Learning should feel magical at times, but teaching is not a magic show. Students are never impressed by the 'slow reveal' – indeed, most find it hugely irritating. Never put a piece of paper over part of an overhead projector slide so that only part of it can be seen until you are ready to reveal the next point. Your default position with a data projector is that *all* of the material should appear on the screen at once unless you have a very good reason to withhold some of the information when you first show the slide. If you want to release information slowly, it is better to produce several slides.

Types and amount of material to use with it

Using a projector (of either sort) makes you feel as if you could include anything on it, but make sure that you use the space wisely. Always use a sans serif font in at least 20-point size, avoid colours that might disappear in bright light (red is notorious for this, while yellow is invisible from a distance in most media), have a simple background and, as much as is reasonable, use separate slides for graphic and written information.

How to use it successfully

Laser pointers frequently make the presenter of the material look a little ridiculous, as there is a temptation to wave the little red dot across the screen to show up every single point being made. Generally speaking, you need only point to some detail on an illustration – your students can read the text and follow your points quite happily.

It takes time for a group of students to take in a new slide, so look at the screen with them when you first show it, read it through yourself so that you are working at a similar speed to the students, then turn back to them, see if they are looking at you or the screen and only begin to talk when the majority of them are looking at you.

As you prepare for a teaching event in which you intend to use a projector, take as your basic premise the need to make slides sparse if they are to be effective. You do not want to be caught having to 'talk through' a slide just because there is too much information on there. Allow the slides to offer your students the key points – from there on it is down to you.

You will need to decide whether or not you want to offer a handout to the students that contains a copy of all the slides. This reveals your entire set of slides before you have even begun to speak and can cause problems if you miss a slide out as you talk. It is, however, a useful, and permanent, resource for the students.

 TOP TIP

Prepare as much as you can before the event. If you are using an overhead projector, make sure that you know where the switches and adjustment handles are and can put the acetate on the projecting surface perfectly straight. Be prepared to switch it off when not using it so that you avoid the students staring into the light like rabbits caught in headlights. If you are using a data projector, prepare blank slides for when you know you will not need images for some time, produce some 'hidden' slides in case the timings go awry and always have back-ups of either acetate or paper copies of your slides. If you are using the internet via a data projector, make the connection to the site before you begin and minimise it so it is ready for the moment when you need it. Connection to the Internet can fail occasionally, so, if this material is a prime part of your session, you might want to save some screenshots in advance, just in case.

The ideal situation for its use

We would tend to use an overhead projector if the teaching room provided no other technology or we wanted to create material with our students during a session, such as in a seminar. Nowadays, overhead projectors are used sparsely, so there is the potential for students to think we are being a bit 'low-tech' when we do use it.

We would use a data projector in a situation when access to images stored on a computer or online access is needed or when we want to give a visually impressive teaching performance. The word 'performance' here is telling: we would usually reserve our use of a data projector to those teaching occasions when we were talking more than interacting, such as lectures. We would encourage our students to use a data projector at some point in a course if they are giving regular presentations, but would ask them to remain open to the possibility of simply talking to get their points across.

THE VOICE OF EXPERIENCE

An important point arose in our discussions with experienced lecturers about projectors:
   'It is worth thinking about your students' total learning experience in any one day. A quick check of their timetable will reveal if they have or are about to experience a run of lectures one after the other. If so, then consider adding some variety to their day. If every other lecturer has produced numerous slides, then if in your session you use more basic materials, it will be a welcome relief.'

TEACHING AND YOUR RESEARCH

Notwithstanding the value of low-tech methods, learning to produce succinct, clear and attractive slides will help you to prepare for presentations of your research at conferences, some parts of which you might prepare for your students as practice for such events.

Interactive whiteboard (smartboard)

What it is/what it does

A fixed electronic whiteboard that allows you to project images on to the screen but also write on it using electronic pens.

Advantages

It allows you to prepare a normal slide presentation and then write all over your slides in response to the students' comments. You also have the option of bringing up blank 'notebook' pages to use as an electronic flipchart. The material produced during the event can be saved and sent to the students or lodged within a virtual learning environment (VLE). Software is available for turning your scribbles into typed text, but it is not always as effective as we would like (at least at present – things may improve), so you will still have to check and edit the text.

TOP TIP

If you intend to write all over a prepared slide presentation, make sure that you have saved a blank copy somewhere else in advance, so that you have two copies – your original for reuse and the amended version for distribution.

Disadvantages

It takes a little time to set up, which is nerve-wracking if a group of students is staring at you in anticipation. Unlike a lecture or seminar for which the notes are on slides ready for a data projector and can easily be printed out in advance in case of disaster, if you are planning a highly interactive session with slides on which you intend notes to be written, the situation is trickier if the technology fails.

Types and amount of material to use with it

The materials that can be used with an interactive whiteboard are almost endless, but that can be a problem. It is best to not get too carried away and throw everything onto it. Students still need you to guide them through the material and inspire them to learn. They also still need you to follow the basic guidelines about font size and so forth that we offered in the previous section on data projectors.

How to use it successfully

Your students will enjoy this teaching aid, as will you, and this makes it worth your while to use it even though it can take some time to get used to exactly what it can do for you.

In case it does not turn out quite as you had expected, it is good to have a 'Plan B' of notes to work from or activities to do that do not involve using all its features. Remember also that your students might have seen it in action rather more than you have. If anything does not work as you had intended, it is perfectly acceptable to ask a couple of members of your student group to share their knowledge of the technology and help you to make it work as you would like. You will not want to lose too much teaching time in this way, but working together with students on technical glitches for a minute or two can be a productive experience in terms of the group dynamic.

WORD OF WARNING

Time spent trying to fix a problem on an interactive whiteboard can seem like it is lasting an eternity when you are trying to teach, but the technology can lead you into some exciting teaching spaces. It allows you to use slides, notes, the Internet and interactive voting systems, but moving from one to another can take time and things might not always go to plan. If you can, schedule a couple of short breaks into your first few sessions with this teaching aid. That way, if things go wrong you can abandon it for a while, but then return to it and try to set everything up during the next break. Then, no teaching time is lost and you will be giving the technology the best possible chance. There is, though, no substitute for carefully practising with the equipment when no one is looking and waiting for you to illuminate their understanding.

The ideal situation for its use

As the above discussion suggests, it might be a good idea to use it in a small group situation first. That way you can try out all of its features with confidence before revealing your abilities to a wider group. It can feel rather cumbersome to write on the board – the pen tends to lag a second behind your movements – but if your students are not very familiar with the system, they may well enjoy the novelty of seeing it in action. As with all technology, have back-ups in place, so, ideally, have a flipchart or standard whiteboard to hand and make sure that you have handouts ready in case of a problem.

TEACHING AND YOUR RESEARCH

There are occasions when, talking about your research with students, they bring a new perspective to bear or make suggestions about how to present it (a useful metaphor, a novel example, a really searching question …) that you would like to record to think about later. This can be done readily when using an interactive whiteboard and it has the added advantage of keeping the note in context with the flow of ideas as they occurred – something that the scribbled paper note may not achieve.

Handouts

What they are/what they do

Handouts are probably as old as teaching itself. They are the guides that help students through a learning situation and the 'take away' material which allows students to look back on the teaching event.

Advantages

They are utterly reliable. You prepare them in advance, make enough copies for the group and know every word contained in them. They are also versatile: students can share handouts if the group is larger than expected; a copy of the handout (amended if you like) can be circulated electronically after the event, either by e-mail or a virtual learning environment; any student needing revision help (or having lost the handout) can be given a further copy, with additional notes written on it if this would help.

Disadvantages

Students can become too reliant on them ('I don't have to think or interact now; I can look at the handout later') and use them in the mistaken belief that a handout replicates a learning event ('I won't go to the lecture; I will pick up a copy of the handout instead'). If this tendency exists (or if you produce unnecessarily detailed handouts), students can find them overwhelming, especially if they are faced with dozens of pages – perhaps hundreds of pages – of undigested handout material in the weeks leading up to an exam.

Although students tend to rely on handouts to give them reliable and authoritative information, they can also find them boring. No data projector display, perhaps no colour at all, just text and plenty of facts. You need not make this your problem, but it is worth being aware of it. Thus, a colourful or more creative handout can be a boost to both learning and the group dynamic in a teaching situation. Compare, for example, the handouts that you devise with the material your students produce if you ask them to give presentations with handouts. If theirs are significantly more professional-looking and enticing than yours, you might want to take this as a hint, however unintentional.

WORD OF WARNING

Sometimes you have to produce supporting information that looks bland on the page but comes to life as you teach, so sometimes your students will just have to have 'boring' handouts. However, this is not the same as *you* becoming bored by your handouts. If you tend to use the same handouts time and time again, you will get bored with the material as you have presented it on the handout and the students will sense this. Also, you may miss out obvious points because you have overused it. Refreshing your occasional handouts at least once a year is a good idea; if you use them frequently an update every term makes sense.

Types and amount of material to use with them

There are three types of handouts: those that only give information, those giving reassurance and those which inspire. Information–giving handouts are the most common type, but do not neglect the others, which are used less often but to good effect. A reassuring handout would offer guidance to the student group – a bulleted list of topics you intend to cover with them in a session or a set of instructions. An inspiring handout might simply contain a picture of the final result of a piece of lab work or a magnificent image reflecting success in a project. If you worry about how much paper this might use, take a hard look at what you are printing off: sometimes a reassuring or inspiring handout is of far greater learning value than a page of information that could be accessed electronically instead.

TOP TIP

The symbiotic relationship between teaching and various teaching aids should not be over-looked. Repeating material from one form of teaching aid to another can be supportive to students, backed up further by you discussing the point in class. It may be, for example, that you choose some key points from a series of slides to produce as a handout as 'take away' material. The easiest way to decide what material to put where is to think of its longevity and the learning experience. What is needed now, what will be needed for coursework assessment, what will be useful for revision?

How to use them successfully

Always think about handouts backwards – that is, not the process of you making them first, but, rather, what happens to them afterwards and where they will end up. If they is aimed to inspire, be as creative as you can. If it is going to be used to reassure, leave plenty of white space on the handout – students always find this reassuring. If it is designed to give information, think about how interactive it will be. If you expect (and want to encourage) students to write their own notes all over it, print it on one side only and leave space for their notes. Indeed, handouts work well if they include enough space for students to write on them during an event, thus making them personalised learning and revision aids.

The ideal situations for their use

Handouts can work well in any situation, but they do take time to distribute and students do actually like to read them, there and then. In a seminar situation, this can be a good way to start things off, giving students a few minutes to read through the material and get their confidence up before they have to speak out.

In a lecture, it can be a hindrance if you find that your audience is looking down when you had hoped for interest and eye contact. It can mean that you simply have to stand there, in silence, waiting for the students to read the handout, while also being acutely aware that a few are not reading it and clearly waiting for you to continue. So, you need to decide in advance how to provide your audience with the handout. Circulating it just before the event is the most efficient way, but it reveals all of your material at once. If you would rather not do this, then you can circulate copies during a mid-event break, if there is one. If you need to hand it out at a particular moment during the event, use the time it takes to circulate it to ask for questions on what you have said so far. That way, nobody is just sitting waiting for the material and doing nothing.

If you choose to circulate copies of your handout at the end of a lecture, you will need to decide how to do it. The most effective way is probably during a final question and answer session, if there is one. A few people might be distracted but this will not be a huge problem. Alternatively, you could leave copies at the back of the room, ideally in several locations, so that the queues to pick them up are not too long. If you are offering handout material at any point other than the beginning of an event, you must state clearly what the handout contains, so as to avoid anxiety or unnecessary notetaking, which can annoy and distract both students and lecturer.

THE VOICE OF EXPERIENCE

It is tempting at the beginning of a teaching career to include in your handouts everything that you intend to say, especially if your students have to sit an exam on your topic and you are worried that you might miss something important out. Although your concern for them is admirable, avoid making this response. Here are some useful suggestions from our experienced colleagues:

'It's usually enough for handouts to provide key words, any difficult to spell words, outlines of processes and so on – the handout can then be a trigger to remember what you told them rather than a substitute for your telling them, making them active rather than passive learners.'

'I like to keep students actively engaged in the session by including in the handout spaces to be filled in by them at certain points in the session – say, the main points during a debate on a topic. This can provide an opportunity to ask them to generate a list of important issues from the session or part of a session. I've found that having a reputation for doing this can help people to concentrate during the session!'

TEACHING AND YOUR RESEARCH

Making a synopsis of your topic is good practice for producing the abstracts of future journal articles or proposals for conference papers, whether or not the topics you teach map well onto your research area.

Virtual learning environment (VLE), including 'Turnitin'

What it is/what it does

A website or series of interconnected websites on which is lodged teaching material and via which a lecturer and students may interact.

  WORD OF WARNING

These online systems are called by a variety of names. Make sure that the system you are using is supported and endorsed by your institution (which will be paying a licence fee for it) and

(Continued)

(Continued)

attend some basic training if you can. The systems are not difficult to use at all, but they have many features that you might like but would not necessarily find easily just by wandering through the site.

Advantages

They can save you a vast amount of time. Once a year, you can trawl through the whole site (or sites) to ensure that out-of-date material has been removed and the up-to-date material is fit for purpose in terms of your next year's teaching. In most cases, the site will simply be 'rolled over' centrally, with the coming year's students automatically being enrolled. If you are running a whole module, it saves you finding and reproducing a hard copy of material such as reading lists each year.

By having access to the site, your students will no longer be reliant on pieces of paper. For example, whenever they are in the library, they can find the book list for an assignment because it is online. It also radically reduces the number of minor queries you receive by e-mail, especially if you add a 'frequently asked questions' section to the site. Similarly, if you need to make an announcement about changes to the teaching structure of the course, such as a cancelled lecture, you can e-mail all of the students and add the announcement to the site, so you can be sure that all students should have been informed.

One huge advantage of the technology we have available to us today is that we can use submission systems such as 'Turnitin'. Students submit their written work electronically (they may still be asked to submit hard copies at the same time) and it is processed by the 'Turnitin' system, which then offers the marker a variety of statistical information on how likely it is that the work includes plagiarised text. This system has the clear advantage of finding potential examples of plagiarism, but its benefit is far greater than this as its very presence in their learning lives makes students more aware of the consequences of plagiarism (even accidental plagiarism caused by carelessness or poor notetaking).

Disadvantages

Students have to assume that everything on the site is accurate and up to date and some find this makes them anxious: they would much rather have a lecture list in hard copy so that they can feel certain that it is correct. The timing of the 'rollover' of information from one student cohort to the next is crucial. For example, if it happens late in the academic year, your new student group may feel at a disadvantage because they did not get their reading list early enough.

Students also sometimes report that they find the whole idea of their studying life intruding into their online social life unpalatable. They are happy to check out online resources when they have chosen to work on an assignment, but the idea that they have to break away regularly from their social network sites to check an educational network site, just in case a lecture time has been altered, can antagonise them.

 TOP TIP

Get to know every nook and cranny of your site, including the archived sections, so that you never overlook anything when you are spring cleaning. Just one inaccurate piece of information that you forgot to remove (such as last year's hand-in date for an assignment) can cause major problems.

Types and amount of material to use with it

Setting up an online resource such as this can be time-consuming to start with, but it will save you time in the long run, provided that you decide in advance how much time you are prepared to spend on it. You can include amazing teaching materials, such as images, film and audio, hyperlinks to any other site, smartboard material that has been created in a classroom and then uploaded, wikis, discussion groups and so on. The list seems fairly endless, but all of it takes time, so it is best to avoid getting too carried away at the outset, then finding that you do not have time to maintain and update the site regularly.

Decide before you begin just how interactive you want to be. A learning site such as this can be valuable in 'static' form, when it is used simply to e-mail students and hold information that is not going to change, such as a reading list, assignment instructions, lecture schedules and links to your departmental handbook and/or style guide. This would need to be updated just once a year and is effectively doing little more than replacing hard copy information with an online equivalent.

In interactive form, you might introduce discussion forums, online assessments and testing, student- or tutor-led wikis, sign-up systems for sessions – pretty much anything you could otherwise do face to face. This type of interactivity allows you and your students to form an online community and teach and learn anytime, but even a student-led wiki or discussion group needs to be monitored to some extent by a tutor, so it is going to eat into your time.

How to use it successfully

Be firm – with yourself and your students. With yourself in terms of having a clear vision of how you want to use the resource and sticking to the amount of time you decide you can spend on it; with your students in not allowing their momentary anxieties to overwhelm your good intentions. If the reading list is lodged online, then there is no need for you also to produce a hard copy – no discussion, no argument.

The ideal situation for its use

An online resource works well in most situations. Indeed, for distance and open learning courses it may be an essential component of the learning. Even for campus-based courses it adds fluidity to learning, from which students and lecturers alike can benefit.

The only time we have seen it fail spectacularly is when lecturers become so enraptured with it that they forget others might not have the right technology to hand in order to use it at all moments in the day. So, for example, if you are giving a lecture during which you are going to refer to material that is on the VLE and you need students to refer to it as you talk, you cannot assume (yet) that every student in the room will have a hand-held electronic device on which they can view the site and make notes. At least for now, hard copy handouts will still be needed at times.

TEACHING AND YOUR RESEARCH

This resource is ideal if you are confident in using electronic media and, indeed, may help you to build up your confidence and repertoire, but it comes into its own when your research can be displayed to advantage in action and visually. The use of imagery in photographic or film form will help you to engage learners (in the classroom or the conference room) in the process as well as the product of research. You can show live creatures (including people), views through a microscope, segments of a play, a dissection in action, chemical reactions, bridges built ... the opportunities are there – the only limits are your imagination and your available time!

Wikis and online polling systems

What they are/what they do

Both of these teaching aids allow students to make their own learning resources in a highly interactive way. A wiki is an online space with set protocols within which students can upload material so as to set up teaching and/or general support resources that can be used by other members of a small group or by the whole student group for a module. It might be part of a VLE or a separate online entity.

An online polling system allows a group of people to respond to an event online using their mobile phones. This builds up an instant resource during the event, but such systems also allow for comments to be sent in after the event, thus increasing the impact of the learning experience over time.

There are two types of online polling systems: those that rely on hand-held electronic devices (sometimes called 'clickers'), which allow students who are physically in the room to press a button and vote, and those which rely on mobile phones and allow students to text in their comments.

Advantages

They are exciting and students are impressed with their interactivity. Wikis allow students to take control of a learning situation to a large extent and they make groupwork easy to view and mark. Online polling systems allow even shy students to speak up and kinaesthetic learners in particular love them. They give you an interesting insight into your students' views and can be used to test where they are in their learning.

Disadvantages

Wikis could theoretically be left to students, but, in reality, students tend not to trust fully what is in them until an academic has looked over the site and checked it all. So you will probably need to take time to do this and let it be known that you will do so.

It would be a brave academic who was prepared to face a lecture hall full of students and then try to use an online polling system with no back-up and no technical support. In all cases where we have seen this system used, it has been a combined effort, with one or two people orchestrating the event up front, while one person is ensuring that the technology works. This is especially useful if you want to monitor texts before allowing them to appear on the screen.

THE VOICE OF EXPERIENCE

The first time one of us experienced the use of Twitter was at a national conference (name removed to save embarrassment) when the audience was requested to comment on or raise questions about the keynote speeches as they occurred. The comments were shown on a screen behind the speakers and were streamed to those who could not attend. This meant that the system was publically accessible. We were all thrilled to be playing with this new technology until some rude tweets, presumably from outside, started to appear above the speakers' heads! This was a learning experience for us all – organisers, presenters and participants alike.

Types and amount of material to use with them

Wikis need to have clearly defined boundaries so that students can work on them with confidence and not spend an unrealistic amount of time on the wiki element of an assignment. The type and amount of material on the wiki will be dictated by the students, but it will help if you are prepared to create a sample wiki to show them before they start on their own.

Although it is possible to see a log of activity on a wiki, and so mark individuals as part of a groupwork assignment, it can be very time-consuming. It is perhaps best to offer a groupwork mark for the wiki and an individual mark for other aspects of a module.

   WORD OF WARNING

The etiquette of a wiki can cause problems. Students might not be used to peer review in this forum and so might criticise one another's contributions too harshly by mistake or be afraid to say anything critical at all. This problem can lead to group disharmony and/or a less impressive wiki than might otherwise have been achieved. It is worth spending time talking about the etiquette of peer review so that students can alter the wiki and make comments with confidence.

Online polling systems can be used to 'open up' a new subject. An hour spent debating an issue (ideally, with two or three people up front actually having a debate), then asking for a response shows students that even academics do not agree on everything in their field and allows the students to show off their knowledge in an area and – equally importantly – ask questions by text that they might hesitate to ask in person.

Online polling also works well if you have any scope in terms of the material you are including in a module. Student engagement can be seen to have been achieved if you are able to ask them to vote for which material they would like to cover for some part of the module. There is some debate currently about the level of student engagement with teaching and learning that is desirable, but, if you favour more student engagement in structuring a module, this is one way to achieve it.

How to use them successfully

For both wikis and online polling systems, the material that is produced will cause you few problems. If any do arise, it is easy enough to amend a wiki and online polling material can be monitored as the situation develops. However, the rate at which material is produced could be a challenge. Wikis can grow huge seemingly overnight and text responses coming in from 120 students to an online poll can be hard to manage.

You need to control the situation as tightly as possible in both of these cases. For a wiki, make it clear early on that you will not be checking the wiki daily but will monitor it periodically and let your students know when this will happen. Also, be clear about the feedback you will offer. Will you actually be correcting the wiki at these times or will you simply offer general feedback about a wiki site and leave the students to make corrections prior to your final visit, when you will ensure that it is absolutely accurate and can be relied on by all?

For online polling, control also comes at the outset. Before any polling begins, make it clear how you will respond to it. You might, for example, tell students that you (and your fellow debaters if this is a team effort) will only be able to respond instantly to the first 5 (or 10 or 20) text responses, but reassure the audience that you will read every single text sent in and respond after the event, via your VLE or in person at a lecture or seminar. You will not necessarily want to respond to each individual text but can talk in a more general way about themes that have arisen and so son.

 TOP TIP

A wiki is an ideal forum for 'legacy work'. One group of students can create a wiki that you then approve and keep on the VLE (crediting those students who created it) ready for use by the next cohort of students. The idea that they are helping others really seems to inspire students to create the best possible wiki.

The ideal situation for their use

While both of these teaching aids can work in a variety of situations, they are used to best effect in situations where communication needs to be enhanced and/or recorded. For this reason, they work well as we have outlined throughout this section, but they are also a useful means of connecting potentially disparate groups, such as part-time learners or distance learners, who can create their own learning environment online. These online opportunities might begin at a summer school, for example, when a group of students could start a wiki while they are physically in the same place and then continue to build on it once they have returned to their disparate locations.

Both wikis and online polling systems can be useful for those students who are working in their second language as they have time to consider before they contribute to the learning situation. They also leave a valuable space for learning in situations where you would like to encourage both immediate and more thoughtful, considered responses to a learning challenge.

TEACHING AND YOUR RESEARCH

Wikis might address areas of your research that generate some debate so you can work through your ideas with a group of students and potentially benefit from their queries, need for elaboration or contributions to the debate that you may not have considered previously. Similarly, using online polling may reveal issues that require further or better explanation before being made more public – particularly to the demanding research community.

Demonstration

What it is/what it does

Any time something in action is shown to students, it is a demonstration. This differs from an example. So, showing how an equation can be resolved on a whiteboard is an example, whereas showing how a dynamo works is a demonstration. The dynamo example is apt here as we tend to think of demonstrations being used more frequently on technical or scientific courses than on arts and humanities courses, for example, although there is no inherent reason for other subject areas not to use them just as happily. For instance, you could demonstrate an interview technique, or how to knot a tie or a rope in an historical or artisan way, or how to use your voice as an actor, or how to perform any kind of action in sport, dance or art work.

Advantages

They are exciting – partly, we must admit, because students think they might go wrong. They also show exactly what you want to show at exactly the right time. There is the adage that a picture is worth a thousand words; a demonstration is probably worth several thousand.

Disadvantages

They can go wrong. This is not necessarily a problem as long as you have a back-up plan – and students will enjoy the moment.

 TOP TIP

It can be a useful aid to teaching – and great fun – to ambush students with a demonstration. On a course when they never see anything other than a lecturer or seminar leader imparting information, introducing a demonstration can wake them up intellectually and keep them on their toes. It does not need to be a demonstration of anything terribly important: in this context, its effect can sometimes be more important than its content.

Types and amount of material to use with it

It is perhaps a shame that the possibility of teaching by using a demonstration is overlooked so often – we would love to see it used far more frequently because of its impact on learning. It is possible for students to study whole modules on Shakespearean texts without once standing up and demonstrating to others how the text actually works in action, simply because their lecturers have not thought of demonstrations as a 'natural' way for them to teach in that field. We would urge you to consider adding this form of learning to your portfolio of teaching aids.

How to use it successfully

Always ask obvious questions about the practicalities first. Are any objects you are going to use easily portable? Will they fit happily into the space available? Will all members of the learning group be able to see the demonstration?

Then think about the interactivity levels. Are you simply going to demonstrate and move on? Are you going to ask some students to try out the demonstration, too? Are you happy to make the objects available for a while so that students can come back and have a go later?

The ideal situation for its use

We are tempted to urge you to favour small-group teaching for demonstrations, as this is likely to be a situation in which all students will be able to see and, if it is useful, interact with the demonstration easily. However, we have seen demonstrations work well in many different teaching situations, so be bold!

Perhaps the situation is less important than your reaction to the demonstration. You might be nervous about whether or not it will work or how well it will be received. Practising the demonstration will obviously help with this, but if you are a natural blusher, you might have to accept that this is an occasion when you will have to blush and ignore it. Practising will also prevent the uncomfortable feeling students get when a demonstrator looks surprised as the demonstration takes place, as if the demonstrator has not bothered to try it out beforehand.

If it *does* go wrong, try to avoid lengthy apologies about it. Comments such as, 'Well, it has always worked before' or 'It was working perfectly this morning' do nothing to aid the situation and simply prolong the moment until you have to move on. Instead, have your back-up plan ready so that you can abandon the 'live' version as soon as you are certain that it is not going to cooperate. Making a quip that life is full of uncertainties and surprises will suffice in most instances to amuse the students and build some rapport.

THE VOICE OF EXPERIENCE

One thing both of us agree on is that it pays not to be so full of your own self-importance as a teacher that you cannot afford sometimes for the joke to be on you. Having – and, what is more, showing – that you, too, have a sense of the ridiculous not only makes learning and teaching enjoyable but also helps boost the confidence of your learners to try out new ideas and activities.

TEACHING AND YOUR RESEARCH

Your research may require large or expensive equipment or access to dangerous, volatile, ephemeral or classified materials or information, but there could well be research activities, processes or skills that you could demonstrate to your students to give them an insight into your research, while at the same time providing you with an opportunity to practise and get some feedback. This is disseminating the research process as well as results, both of which are important.

Film and audio

What they are/what they do

Film clips or audio recordings (which you have made yourself or are already on CD or DVD) that you show to or share with students using a variety of means (as part of a slideshow, via a data projector, a virtual learning environment or an online film clips site, for example).

Advantages

They can enliven a teaching situation and keep your students alert. They also save you time in that one film or audio clip can demonstrate a point well without the need for lengthy explanations.

Disadvantages

Although they can save you descriptive time, they can take an unexpectedly long time to set up and play. Always factor into your timing the space you will need to set up the clip and play it in full.

TOP TIP

Avoid planning to use a video or audio clip at the very end of a session. Although it can seem like a perfect way to wind down a learning situation, in reality students might spend the time surreptitiously packing up their things rather than concentrating. Also, if you have run over slightly on time, there will always be the temptation to show the clip even though you know that it will make the session run over and students will not forgive this lightly, nor will those waiting outside to use the room next.

Types and amount of material to use with them

The main decision to make is whether these are to be permanent or ephemeral teaching aids. That is, are you only going to show them in the teaching situation or also lodge them on the Internet (either publically or in a virtual learning environment) so that students can revisit them repeatedly? Once you have made this decision, make sure that all of the students are aware of the availability.

How to use them successfully

As with a demonstration, you will need to practise enough to feel confident about using the technology and the material itself. Then, you will need to consider how much 'additional learning' is required. It is rare for a video or audio clip to do all of the work for you, but it is too easy to slip into a general discussion about what you have all just seen or heard, with the risk that you might miss some important points. If general discussion and student feedback is what you hoped to evoke by using the material, you might want to consider offering a handout at the end of the session with some key learning points.

 WORD OF WARNING

Students can find it surprisingly difficult to listen to an audio clip alone – try showing them a static image at the same time. They will often hear better if they can see something.

The ideal situation for their use

As with a demonstration, check that the situation suits the purpose. How large is the room? Will all the students be able to see and hear? Are the blinds working?

Remember to consider the light levels in the room. There is often an assumption that you need to pull down the blinds for every viewing situation whereas, in reality, often, for a short clip, natural light or even turning the lights on, is not going to hinder the viewing. Turning the lights off and fiddling about with curtains and blinds takes time and can be a distraction, so only do it if you really need to.

As with a demonstration, have a Plan B ready in case of disaster. It is easy enough to lodge a film or audio clip in several electronic locations so that you can access it in some version on the day. There is no need to be put off by file size. Your institution should have a system that allows you to lodge clips on the VLE – just make sure that the loading and buffering times are not off-putting.

If you have planned to use a DVD or CD and it fails to work on the day, check out online film and audio clip sites and you will probably find the clip you need is there, causing minimal disruption to the flow of your teaching.

TEACHING AND YOUR RESEARCH

If your research experience falls into a category that makes it difficult to demonstrate live (it is dangerous, involves large equipment or animals, infectious materials), then it may be that you could make a film of it to include in your session or there may be archive films of a relevant process. Even a small extract can bring to life some area of your research that may seem dry if put into words or may be difficult to explain. If you decide to go to the trouble of making a film clip, consider a topic that might usefully also be included in a conference presentation or a presentation to your funders to make the effort doubly worthwhile.

Online resources and mobile phones

What they are/what they do

Online resources are materials accessed via the Internet and used either in a teaching situation or by students when they are learning. We would also include here the possibility of online blogs created by students or by others.

Mobile phones are mentioned here as one of us was recently surprised by technology during a seminar. The perfectly sourced material would have been splendid had the university's Internet system not crashed at the vital moment. The material was not essential to the session and so had not been taken offline and saved, but it was irritating to lose the chance to view it nevertheless. Imagine the delight when a resourceful student pointed out that every student in the room had access to a phone with Internet provision, so they could all look at the material regardless. It was a great moment of shared learning and, although we would not recommend it as a regular practice, it is worth bearing in mind.

Advantages

Students are familiar with the Internet, it can be accessed by them from anywhere in the world and contains a vast amount of useful material.

Disadvantages

Students are familiar with the Internet and so segue on to social networking sites when they are supposed to be studying. It can be accessed from anywhere, so you might have no control over the learning taking place (not that this need always be a bad thing). It contains a vast amount of useful material ... and an awful lot of rubbish!

 WORD OF WARNING

Although you can presume that students will all have Internet access – assuming your institution gives them this opportunity – you cannot assume that they have access at all times of the day and night. Although we know that most students have Internet access via their laptops or phones, it would be unreasonable to ask them to complete an assignment online or source material overnight, thus not giving them enough time to access the resources available within your institution.

Types and amount of material to use with them

Varying the sources on which you rely helps to keep your students interested. So, rather than always suggesting the Internet, remember to encourage students to use books and journals (not all of which are available on the Internet or as e-books, of course) and remind them that face-to-face contact can sometimes be more productive than relying on an Internet discussion group for study.

How to use them successfully

Be precise about what you expect your students to extract from the Internet. Give students plenty of guidance on the pitfalls of using the Internet as an academic tool (they are still remarkably naïve about its value), simply 'ban' certain sites if you know they will be misleading and try to achieve a balance between giving them some site addresses and encouraging them to use their own judgement.

 TOP TIP

In a small group, it is possible to volunteer to vet sites for students before they rely on them too heavily. This is not entirely altruistic – they will be doing plenty of legwork and giving you a useful list of online resources as they go.

The ideal situation for their use

The answer here seems obvious: any situation when you are not there to teach them face to face, but we would challenge this thinking. Students often see using the Internet for study as a solitary pursuit when, at best, they might have some 'virtual company' in a study discussion group or chatroom. The problem with this is that they can be uncertain about how to use the Internet wisely and you would be unaware of the problem, as you are not in a position to get a face-to-face response from them as they look through any online resources you have created. If you can use online resources in your teaching sessions from time to time you will be sharing at least the medium of this kind of learning with them, which can offer benefits in terms of both their learning and your teaching.

TEACHING AND YOUR RESEARCH

Although we would never advocate using your students to do your work for you, it may be that exercises in which they seek information from the Internet about a topic will reveal sites that you have missed yourself. Some of us are less experienced with, and have less time for, roaming the Internet than do some students. The sites they find may contain useful information for your research or about similar research or may have misleading information that you need to be alert to so you can refute it. This can produce learning in action for us all.

EXERCISE 14

There is no reason to suppose that you would be a better educator just by using lots of teaching aids. On the other hand, it is nice to know you are not missing out by overlooking an aid that would substantially improve the learning experience you are offering. The chart here allows you to record your experiences with teaching aids in the course of the coming months or years.

Teaching aid	When used	Group size and topic area	Why it was used	Did it work?

By looking back over your entries on this chart in the future, you will be reminded of your successes and, most probably, of other times when a teaching aid you used was not the best choice. It will, we hope, inspire you to keep a variety of teaching aids in your teaching repertoire.

Students

You might reasonably be wondering why we have included students here. We opened this chapter by stating that you are your best teaching aid. Well, your students come a close second.

Their gratitude keeps you going on a bad day when you almost forget why it is you teach. Their frowns of confusion tell you that what you thought was a perfect explanation is not working at all. Their apathy can make you even more determined to transform their learning experience. Then, when they are generous enough to share their moments of enlightenment with us, when they are excited enough to let us share their space for learning, we know that it is all worthwhile.

Eight
HANDLING ASSESSMENT

The assessment process can be intimidating for anyone new to it. This is understandable. Your teaching life is, to a great extent, private to you and your students. If you do not quite finish all you want to do in a session, nobody will mind; if you need to look something up and get back to your students, they will understand; if you want to try out a new way of doing things, there are only your learners there to judge you. As an assessor, you can feel exposed in every judgement you make. Your marks are precisely tied to one specific piece of work and a colleague might challenge that mark, which, in itself, is a nerve-wracking thought, however good you feel about a mark you have given.

 WORD OF WARNING

Before we even begin to work through the process of marking with you, there is one crucial point to keep in your mind whenever you are marking anything. Your students are not you, so judge them by the general standard that is expected and/or achieved, not by your recollection of what you think you could have achieved at their stage of education – your memory is bound to be inaccurate.

Added to this, you will find that your role feels reversed in some ways. Until this point, you have been giving out the information and the inspiration, which is satisfying and exciting, even if it is challenging at times. Now you are powerless: all you can do is sit back and see the result. Until you become very used to marking, you can feel unnerved by this. You desperately want your students to do well – not just for their sakes, but because their work reflects your teaching – yet there is nothing you can do.

The reflection on your teaching can become burdensome as you mark because human nature will naturally lead you to notice any blunder and wonder if a student has got it wrong or if you somehow gave him or her the wrong impression. Your advice will also come back to haunt you. For example, you advised a group to structure their work in a certain way and they did not produce particularly impressive work. It is not your fault, but you will probably feel guilty. The spotlight on you does not end there. You will be involved in writing assessed essay questions and examination papers and these will be scrutinised as they go through the system. It is not just your students who are being judged.

Although most of the work you mark will be submitted to you anonymously, this is unlikely to stop you recognising the odd student (or thinking that you do) from the topics they have chosen or their writing style. If you think some work has been produced by a normally excellent student and yet it is mediocre, it can leave you feeling deflated.

You will be judging the initial mark for a piece of work by yourself and this can be a lonely moment. Although you will compare many of your marks later, that first judgement is not made alongside a supportive colleague, it is yours alone. What you are judging may feel very familiar to you (part of what your students are giving back to you is what you gave them in the first place), but there are times when the material is far less familiar.

Alongside the work of your own students, you may be asked to mark the work of students on modules and courses other than your own. If you have taken a seminar group in a large module, you will be marking the assignments from students in that module, but often not the work of your own seminar group.

 WORD OF WARNING

The practicalities of the assessment process can never be taken lightly. Do not allow yourself to be drawn into giving out information that might be inaccurate. If a student catches you in the corridor or sends you a chatty but complicated e-mail about his or her work that includes a brief question about a submission date, the format of an examination or such like, always refer that student back to official documentation or the examinations officer.

You will notice that we have entitled this chapter 'handling assessment', which we think reflects another aspect of marking that you might find challenging – that it is a process. You receive students' work, usually in batches, then you have to make a fairly speedy decision about that work, to a deadline, and pass it on. It may be marked by a colleague, too, which could lead to a discussion of the mark and it might be changed before being entered on to a system, ready to be judged, perhaps, by external examiners before being assessed as a 'run of marks' for that student … and you have to do this again, and again, and again.

THE VOICE OF EXPERIENCE

We hope it reassures you to know that it is not unusual for first and second markers to disagree. Some of our experienced colleagues noted that sometimes there is a complete divergence of opinion about work that involves creative or reflective responses rather than calculation or factual descriptions. This is one of the reasons examination boards employ external examiners. Their first task is to ensure consistency across the discipline and across different institutions, but another is for them to adjudicate between divergent internal markers.

In among all of this it might suddenly hit you: this is what it was all about. The effort you put into your learning events, the enthusiasm shared with your students, the eureka moments and the hard slog, and now it is nearly all over, reduced to this piece of assessment. Of course, this is not true – education is far more than simply a mark awarded for a piece of work – but it is certainly a major part of what we are all here to do and, at the moment of assessment, you can be sure that it is all the student cares about. What pressure.

Do we sound gloomy enough yet? We hope so, because we want to recognise with you that this is not just an additional aspect of your teaching life – it is hard and rather scary at times, which often goes unremarked on and apparently unnoticed. All academics can find their first (and their twenty-first) batch of exam scripts or coursework assignments a challenge, but they tend not to talk about it. That is why we think this is an important chapter in our aim to support you as your teaching career progresses.

Having started on such a downbeat note, we should confess that we both enjoy marking. In talking through this chapter we have been wondering why this is the case, as we know that some academics groan at the very sight of the next batch of assignments to mark. We think it is, at least in part, because we found it so difficult at the beginning of our careers. We agonised over all the aspects of marking we have mentioned so far in this chapter, but persevered. We found our own ways to do things, accepted and came to enjoy the rhythm of marking and became much more confident in our ability to judge the work that we see.

 TOP TIP

Although it will take a while for you to find your perfect marking rhythm and routine, have it in mind as soon as you start to mark, so that you can be looking out for what works best for you.

We also found, in time, the right 'space for marking'. You, too, will need to find this space – the time of day that suits you best, the location, the amount of time you spend marking before you take a break and so forth. This will be important as time goes on and we realise that those colleagues of ours who find marking most burdensome have never developed a rhythm for marking.

One of us (and we will never say which one) gets no further than the kettle before she marks each day. She works her way through the first batch or two of essays with a large cup of tea, settles her mind on the marking process, gets a good sense of what the day's marking is likely to bring and only then does she shower and face the rest of the marking day. Another of us sets her study space up with a flask of coffee, jug of water, a selection of nibbles, a comfy chair and a straight back chair (to vary position) then switches off e-mail and telephone ready to hibernate for the day with her marking.

 EXERCISE 15

You will not want to be too rigid about the time and space you use for marking, but it can be useful to gain a sense of what works for you. Surprisingly, many academics fail to do this and so have to suffer very irregular marking experiences, sometimes feeling good about the process and sometimes feeling deflated and indecisive. As you get into your stride with the next batch of marking you are required to carry out, make a note of the time of day you did some marking, how long you stayed with the task and give it a mark out of ten for how much you enjoyed it/found it satisfying. After some time, you might expect to spot a pattern emerging, revealing which is the best time for you to mark and how long you can mark in one stretch before you lose your impetus and start to struggle.

TEACHING AND YOUR RESEARCH

From these descriptions of the marking process, you may recognise some commonality with research – the importance of immersion in the data in order to recognise patterns and preserve some consistency of interpretation. Pattern recognition is a highly skilled activity, so it is well worth practising at every available opportunity.

Before we explore with you the various aspects of handling assessment, we thought you might like us to explain some terms, just in case they are not familiar to you yet. If you turn to the back of the book, you will find a glossary of assessment terms – you might want to browse through them now. In the glossary we have covered a wide range of terms and there is good reason for this. In our experience it is ignorance of the terminology that embarrasses and confuses otherwise potentially competent and enthusiastic markers. We can both recall moments in our early careers when terms were used that we did not understand and we have also been in meetings where we have had to stop proceedings in order to explain to a colleague what a term means.

In the rest of this chapter we will point out some techniques and pitfalls of assessment, as well as nodding towards some of its pleasures, but we are aware that you will develop in your own way as an assessor. Despite our gloom earlier, this is an art, an art that you may come to enjoy very much as your experience grows. Every academic is unique in the way they approach this area and that is how it should be.

A special note about evaluation

For all teachers it is important to find out whether or not our experiments with teaching are producing the learning that we anticipate. Although at first it may seem daunting to ask your students to evaluate your teaching, perhaps by commenting on the content and presentation, you will probably agree that they are really the only ones who can provide feedback on what it was like to attempt to learn from your session/s. In addition to informing your teaching practice, such feedback also demonstrates to them that we feel accountable for our work.

As much can be said about evaluation as about assessment. Indeed, they have much in common as each can be formative as well as summative, formal or informal, imposed or voluntary. You should check with your department whether or not there are particular customs or rules about the kind and frequency of evaluation and if there are particular formats to be used or if you can devise your own to inform your personal reflection on your practice.

Seen as a development tool, it can aid the enhancement of your teaching skills and indicate to your students that you do indeed care about the quality of their learning experience.

The marking rhythm

We have already suggested that you will find a routine of marking that suits you best, but be aware also of your natural rhythm. Although you will have a set of criteria so that you know what you should be looking for in a piece of work, you will find that, if you let it happen, marking can be a creative and enjoyable process. You rapidly get a feel for the answer you are expecting and will be working on intuition. This intuition is not just a woolly feeling about what you like but a clear understanding of what is required. You may find that you only become aware of the formal criteria once more *after* you have awarded a mark, when you come to check what you have done.

THE VOICE OF EXPERIENCE

Each of us begins the process of marking in different ways. Some of our colleagues said that they like to read very quickly through a sample of assignments or even all of them before beginning to mark individual ones. This might then result in preparing little piles of scripts that fall into a range of marks before working on each heap in turn to sort them again into a more specific order. Others read each script and make notes about their value, perhaps ordering them from poor to excellent across the floor. Others simply mark each one and move on, only returning to the batch if comparison becomes necessary. You might find it useful to experiment with a range of techniques to find which suits you (and your room space) best.

Be ready for your mark for a piece of work to change as you work through an examination script or assignment. You will run through a range of emotions, from irritation if a comment is wildly inaccurate, disappointment if a student has slightly misunderstood something or excitement when a brilliant opening is offered to delight when it all comes together well and the student soars. This is normal, so let it happen. You might also run through a very wide range of marks in your mind as you work through a piece, but that is an inherent part of the process, too.

You need to get into your stride with each new batch of marking. You may find that you are overly generous or too harsh as you work through the first few pieces in a batch, but you can easily correct these fluctuations when you come to look back at the run of marks as a whole. If you are unsure of a mark, it can be useful at that stage to make direct comparisons between two pieces of work so as to check the accuracy of your marking.

 TOP TIP

The work of international students may knock you off your stride slightly, as their use of English might feel a little awkward and you may inadvertently be tempted to award a lower mark as a result of this. It is for this reason that some academics prefer to mark the work of any international students in a cohort separately, at the end of a marking session. At this point, remember that the purpose of assessment is to check understanding and intellectual ability. If understanding is evident *despite* a lack of elegant English, then this needs to be recognised. See also the discussion below about whether or not to deduct marks for presentation.

Marking criteria

Although your judgement will be the finely honed appreciation of an academic, it is worth knowing at the outset what general criteria might apply. For example, does your department take off a specific number of marks for underlength or overlength work? Are you expected to penalise for poor use of English – and how harsh should the penalty be? If you do notice especially problematic use of language or severe organisational difficulties, are you expected to record a 'reserve' mark in case the student is subsequently diagnosed with dyslexia and so be entitled to have earlier work reassessed?

In addition to general criteria, there might be criteria specific to the module or course on which you are marking, such as every candidate having to show evidence of independent research in an area or each piece of assessment needing to cover certain topics or areas. All of this will be in your mind as you mark.

 WORD OF WARNING

Although there are official marking criteria to be borne in mind, there are also matters of personal taste and belief that you may be surprised to come across as you work with others in the process of moderating or second marking. These might include questions around how much

(Continued)

(Continued)

secondary material should be included, whether or not using plentiful quotations in examinations is necessary and how much the length of a bibliography matters. Academics often feel strongly about these issues so, whether you do or not, be prepared to fight your corner.

Setting examination questions

The first thing you will want to do as you approach setting an examination paper is find every available past paper for the module or course. That way you will avoid repeating previous questions (a problem if the students have access to the past paper on which they appeared, especially if this has been the focus of discussion in tutorials) and you will see how others have approached the task.

Then consider how you would expect a candidate to answer the question. It is so easy to get carried away with a question that you are really enjoying creating, thinking it will open up interesting areas, forgetting that a student might miss those interesting areas and be completely flummoxed by the question or all of your students might flock to the question thinking it is easy but it is in fact the one most likely to trip them up. Of course, you cannot prevent these situations entirely, but considering an examination paper from the recipient's point of view will help.

Keep calm. When you are first asked to write an exam paper or contribute a question to one, you may well be struck by the enormity of the task. This paper will sit in the archives for many years; students' degree classifications might depend on the questions they are given; you might be boosting them up or causing them to crumple in despair in an examination. All of these thoughts might go through your mind as you write the paper or question. This is good, in that it is a serious responsibility and should be approached as such, but not good if it freezes you up totally. Take heart. We have sat in dozens of examiners' meetings and we know from experience that the intellects of students are resilient – whatever is thrown at them, they tend to end up with the right classification level.

THE VOICE OF EXPERIENCE

Our experienced colleagues had different personal ways of devising questions, very few of them starting with a question in mind then worked out what the answer should be. Instead, they suggested working backwards by first focusing on a topic that the students should know about. That topic can then be broken down into its component key aspects, aspects that they should be able to demonstrate knowledge of or work with in a response. Then the task is to consider what question might elicit those points/ideas. All of them had found from experience that it is essential to check carefully that the words used match what the students are expected to do. One colleague said:

'If you are expecting critical reflection rather than a description, then make that clear in the stem of the question.'

Those who prefer this way of developing questions also noted that it means you are beginning with the marking criteria rather than trying to devise them post hoc.

Once any exam paper or question that you have written has been used, always check to see how it was used. Did the students in general spread their answers evenly across the paper or was one question a firm favourite? Was one question avoided altogether? Did most students misunderstand the point of one question? The answers to these questions will not necessarily cause you to change the way you approach the next examination paper, but you need to be sure that you are giving them the fairest possible chance to shine.

 TOP TIP

Marking examination scripts feels very different from marking other forms of assessment. They are written in the instant, usually with no reference to secondary sources and to a strict deadline. This means that they might be unfinished or poorly presented. With an examination script, you make allowances all the time for this circumstance, while still trying to assess the essential worth of the work. For this reason, it makes sense to mark examination scripts in a different marking session to the one in which you mark other forms of assessment, if time allows.

Moderation and double marking

The system of moderating and/or double marking will be specific to the institution and department in which you are working, but there are some guidelines we can offer that will apply to most situations.

- Be sure in advance if this is 'blind double marking', as this will mean not revealing your mark until your colleague has also come up with a mark independently.
- Once you know there will be a discussion around a mark, be clear as to why and how you reached the mark you have given.

- You will be required to give a consensus mark, rather than just 'split the difference', so you might want to decide what your highest or lowest possible mark would be before you meet with the other marker.
- Having said that, be open to persuasion. It might be you have a fundamental disagreement that cannot be resolved, but it could just be one of you has overlooked a point of merit (or demerit) in the work.
- Try not to be intimidated by the fact that another marker might be vastly more experienced than you. You might expect to bow to his or her experience to some degree – that is only logical – but your opinion is still valid and should be heard.
- If you have to go to a third marker for adjudication, make sure that you both agree on the person to be approached to do this.
- If the third marker does not agree with you, accept this gracefully.
- As a matter of courtesy, it is good practice to follow the social niceties of the situation, especially when you are new to marking – meeting at a time convenient to the other markers, thanking them for their input and guidance and so on.

Our experience of double marking has occasionally been frustrating. As we talked through this topic, we could both instantly remember a handful of students (one from more than a decade ago) whose work we think was more accurately marked by us than either the second or third marker. We recognise, however, that everyone has had this experience and just because we still feel the frustration does not mean we were necessarily right. Despite these instances, our overall experience has been a positive one. We enjoy the sense of camaraderie, the insight we get into our colleagues' modules and the reminder that we all care passionately about our subject and the teaching of it.

THE VOICE OF EXPERIENCE

Although we have presented assessment as a separate chapter, it is not really a distinctly separate part of teaching and it certainly contributes to our own learning as teachers. All of our experienced colleagues agreed that marking assignments or examinations gives them an opportunity to gain insight into common misunderstandings or misinterpretations within their subject domains and the ideas that excite and energise students so that they can then use this to inform further teaching. One of us remembers well the shock of realising that the analogies which had helped her understand an abstract idea are now old-fashioned and merely serve to confuse students of today who have lived through different experiences and so are familiar with neither the abstract concept nor the more concrete example to which it used to be likened. Ah, the penalties of becoming 'too experienced'!

Written feedback

When you come to give any written feedback on a piece of work – from a note at the end of an examination answer to a full page (or more) of a cover sheet for an assignment – you need first to be aware of its purpose. Is it to be read by the student or is it an internal note for another assessor and/or the external examiners?

Once you have answered this question, the rest is common sense. If two or more markers are giving written feedback that will be seen by a student, they need to ensure that their comments will not confuse him or her, but also reflect whatever is the final, agreed mark rather than be an indication of variance in the assessment of the piece. Given that a student could appeal against any decision, it is a good idea to be meticulous in your record keeping regarding such notes and marks.

 TOP TIP

Remember that students compare notes, so make sure that you resist the temptation to fall back on repeated, generic comments in your notes to them. You would not expect to make every comment sheet absolutely original – after all, some comments will naturally apply to many students – but be aware of the disappointment that they will feel if it looks like they are seen as 'just one of a batch'. Try to make your comments constructive and open. Where time/space/the material allows, tell the student how something could be improved, rather than simply criticising what is there, and make comments that are clear but allow for some further discussion, should the student come to see you about the piece of work.

Tutorials

In this instance, we are taking tutorials to be meetings between a marker and a single student or a pair or small group of students, meetings that are convened purely to talk through an assessed piece of work. This is a delicate situation and one that you will want to handle with care. Students feel vulnerable when they are discussing their efforts face to face and in detail, yet this is an excellent opportunity to make real changes to their understanding of a subject and encourage them to improve the ways in which they articulate their ideas.

Voluntary or compulsory tutorials?

Find out if your department insists on compulsory tutorials with every student for every piece of work (some see it as one part of a pastoral care system). If they are not compulsory, talk to your colleagues to gain their views before making your own decision. Some academics prefer students to sign up to tutorials on the basis that they would rather spend more time with a few students who have asked for help than simply seeing everyone. Others feel that seeing everyone gives them the best chance to help students, some of whom might not recognise that they need help.

One or several students?

You might decide to see several students at once if you feel there are general points you need to make that apply to them all. This could save you time, but keep in mind that it might inhibit students from asking a question if it seems to be too revealing or trivial. On the other hand, seeing students individually might be intimidating for some of your students, however friendly you are. We have noticed that our colleagues tend to aim for maximum effect by seeing students in groups for some pieces of work and individually for others.

You also need to consider how you feel about this option. If you know that you would find either a one-to-one or group situation rather daunting, you might want to ease yourself into the system slowly to start with by creating the situation that is most comfortable for you.

Frequency of tutorials

You might not want to see every student as a result of every single piece of work. Again, find out what your department's policy is, then make a decision based on your best judgement as to what would help the students and what it is reasonable for them to expect from you by way of one-to-one support.

Written or verbal delivery of an assessed piece?

It is the custom in some institutions for students to read their work aloud during a tutorial and the academic to comment on the piece without having seen it beforehand. This is very much an individual choice. It can save some time, perhaps, and the drama of it appeals to some. It also means that students have to come to see you in order to present their work and gain feedback. On the other hand there is no written record of the feedback and it could be a huge challenge for some students.

As with other aspects of tutorials, you could be allowed to judge for yourself which you feel is the best option, although, to begin with, you will likely follow the well-trodden path walked by your colleagues.

Immediate or considered feedback?

Some educators prefer to give written feedback to allow students to consider their responses prior to a tutorial. Others present a feedback sheet at the time or simply give verbal feedback on the spot.

You will probably know instinctively which method you would prefer to use. You should then give some consideration to the level and nature of the student group and which form would suit the stage that they have reached in their learning process, their maturity and the needs they may have in relation to the course as a whole.

 EXERCISE 16

There can be a danger in tutorials that what was meant to be a helpful and free-flowing discussion of a piece of work actually becomes a mini-lecture about the piece or (even worse) a mini-lecture that has little to do with the work in question. If you think that this might happen to you, you might try a different system from that of simply working through the comments you wrote on a piece of work. Instead, as you mark each student's work, make a note of no more than six key words that sum up the main points you would like to make if that student comes to see you. That way you will avoid taking up precious time simply repeating what you have written and, instead, give more or an overview. This will also leave more time for the students to ask questions and make additional points. This technique will not necessarily work for everyone, so see this as an exercise that you try once to see if it is useful for you.

Making a difference

Although you can see that you have many choices available when it comes to how you run a tutorial, the purpose of this learning event remains the same: to offer feedback and suggest ways in which your students can improve and move forward in their thinking and learning. With this in mind, it is important to move forward from a shared starting point. The starting point would most usually be some written feedback, either a detailed analysis on a cover sheet or some comment written on a piece of work.

Your role in the move forward is to take the student from this starting point to other areas. While you will want to answer any questions a student has about the feedback you have already given, there is little to be gained from simply repeating the feedback. Instead, try to take the opportunity to create a space for learning in a tutorial, space where you can explore with a student the ways in which the work might have gone had there been the chance to develop it further. You might also use the time to consider the learning gained from the module as a whole.

Do not be surprised if students go off the point altogether. You may be asked all sorts of questions about their progress, about their learning plans or their long-term aspirations. Let this happen – the tutorial is their time to confide, their chance to be corrected, but also to be reassured and inspired.

One of us has just been recalling her first ever tutorial. She received an essay mark of 66. Now she knows that this was a firm mid-2:1 mark, but that was not at all the impression she received at the time. She came away from the tutorial sure that she had the potential to get a first and somehow one mark above a 65 was proof. This might, perhaps, have been naïve, but it was rather inspirational all the same. It is a poignant memory as the marker left the university the following year and disappeared from view, so the opportunity to thank her for that first piece of aspirational marking has never presented itself.

CONCLUSION

We were pleased to note that our last sub-heading before this one happens to be 'making a difference' and that we were able to finish with a personal anecdote. That is because this is really what teaching in higher education is about. It is more than a job; it is personal – a giving away of something of yourself and your research in order to change lives, to make a difference. It is also, as we hope we have shown, a chance to use the opportunities around you to interrogate your own work and improve your life as a researcher.

Students all over the country will be graduating every year for the rest of your working life. They will all have increased their knowledge, skills and experience during their time at university. *Yours* can be some of the lucky students who have done more than this, the ones who have received an education in the broadest and most profound sense of the word. They will always remember you as 'their lecturer', the one who made them feel special however many other students you had to teach, and their gain will also be yours.

GLOSSARY OF ASSESSMENT TERMS

Anonymised marking   As the term suggests, this is the practice of marking each piece of work with no idea of the candidate's identity. The only reference you will be given is an examination number or student number (these will be different). The practice of anonymised marking might persist throughout the assessment process, the names of the students only being revealed once a final mark for an entire programme has been agreed.

Blind double marking   A process by which each marker assesses work independently and decides on a suitable mark before comparing notes and marks in order to agree a consensus mark.

Class mark   Although students will receive individual marks, they will be given an overall class of degree (first, upper second (2:1), lower second (2:2), third, pass). You will be aware of this already, but it takes on a different dimension when you are marking because the class mark – the mark that indicates the class of degree awarded – is all. If, for example, the difference between your judgement and that of a colleague is three marks, this might be a fairly minor problem, but if the difference goes across a class mark – that is, will result in a lower class of degree being awarded – the situation is far more fraught. This is one of the reasons why some institutions discourage or even place an outright ban on the awarding of certain borderline marks, such as 39 or 59.

Coursework   Pieces of work produced during a course. These pieces may be referred to as a coursework project, an assignment or a module essay.

Diagnostic assessment   This would usually take place to see where a student's learning might go next. This would be the case if a student undertook a learning needs analysis, for example, or if certain criteria must be met before a student can be admitted to a particular module or course.

Dissertation and thesis   A lengthy piece of written work produced as the result of independent research on the part of a student or researcher. The term 'dissertation' might be reserved for undergraduates and Master's-level students and 'thesis' for doctoral researchers, but this is by no means universally the case. In fact, in the USA, for instance, the terminology is reversed, with a dissertation being one of the products of the doctoral process.

Double credit   Students may be prohibited from writing about the same material between one piece of assessed output and another (perhaps, for example, between coursework and an exam). In some cases, this prohibition is broad (for example, a student who wrote an assessed essay on *Pride and Prejudice* would not be allowed to write on Jane Austen in the exam), but usually it is more specific (the student could not write a second time on *Pride and Prejudice*, but could write on other Austen novels). The way in which the issue of double credit is viewed varies markedly from one institution to another, so you will need to know what the practice is in your institution.

Double marking   All of the assessed material for a module or course is marked by two markers in order to have each mark confirmed. The work might then also be viewed by external examiners.

Evaluation   A systematic review of processes and experiences of learning and teaching to judge their value to different participants or stakeholders so as to inform their improvement and development.

Exam script   An exam answer, or series of them, usually written in an exam booklet produced by your institution.

Examination type   You will be familiar with what is usual for your own field, but it is worth bearing in mind that you have many options when it comes to examination type – short answer, full essay, mixed and multiple choice being just a few.

Examinations officer   Usually, an academic in a department who has been given the task of implementing and overseeing the examination process. Several examinations officers might be appointed so that different cohorts of students are adequately covered.

External examiners Your institution does not carry the weight of assessment alone. External examiners are visiting academics from other institutions who will view the work produced by your students, assess your marking process and sample the work to ensure that the marking is a fair reflection of the work being produced. External examiners will also make comment on the teaching that has produced the assessed work. This is to assure consistency of quality across institutions providing similar courses.

Fieldwork report, essay or submission The result of any work that has been completed outside the institution, such as a placement or time spent abroad.

Formative work Any work that is assessed, but the mark for which does not count towards the final mark for a module or course.

Learning journal Sometimes also called a 'reflective journal', this is a piece of work produced most usually during the period of a course of learning and assessed as either a formative or summative piece of work.

Marking criteria A set of criteria by which a piece of assessed work is to be marked. These may or may not be shared with the candidates.

Moderation Also called sampling, for which a selection (random or otherwise) of the material being assessed is marked also by a second marker who is looking to confirm either individual marks or the level of marking overall or both.

Open and closed book examinations For most examinations, students are alone with their knowledge (closed book), but, on occasion, they are allowed to take specific texts into the examination room with them. There will also be examinations when students are allowed to take other aids in with them.

Oral examination This differs from a viva in that the student is being assessed on oral skills – usually language skills, but sometimes pubic speaking or rhetorical abilities.

Peer review A situation in which students assess the performances of other students. This assessment is not normally included in the formal mark for a module or course, but it could be.

Practical While this term traditionally applied to work completed on courses of study that have a strong practical element (science, fine art), it is becoming increasingly widespread for students in traditionally 'write assessment' subject areas to be given the chance to be assessed for some portion of their overall mark by means of practicals, such as assessed presentations or performances. This term is evolving.

Rubric   The formal instructions given to students about to undertake an assessed piece of work (coursework or examination).

Run of marks   The marks students achieve for their various pieces of work are judged alongside each other – the run of marks – in order to determine an overall mark. The run of marks for a module or course will also be checked to ensure that there are no anomalies in the system.

Sampling   See *Moderation*.

Seen and unseen examinations   Most examination papers will be entirely new to a student, but there are some situations when students will be shown the paper before an examination so that they can prepare in advance. This provides a halfway point between a coursework-only module and one that includes an examination in its means of assessment.

Self-assessment tests   Often now carried out online, these tests are formative in nature and are available for students to judge their own progress.

Step marking   Markers might be not only encouraged to choose a firm class category but also sometimes cajoled or instructed to make a clear distinction between the work of students in a class. This can lead to step marking, which is the awarding only of certain marks in a class. Thus, for example, all students awarded a first in a cohort would have to be given 72, 75, 80, 85 and so on, other marks being out of use. This is a hugely contentious issue in higher education and the debate about the use of step marking is likely to rage for some time to come.

Summative work   Work produced to assess the result of a student's learning – assessed essays, coursework assignments and examinations.

Termly/semester essay   A formative piece of work produced at some point during a module so that the student can gain feedback before producing final coursework or entering an exam. It might also be called a practice essay or (rather bizarrely) a non-assessed essay.

Third marker   A colleague brought in to arbitrate if two markers cannot agree.

Tutorial   Although this term is used slightly differently from institution to institution, we have most usually seen it used to refer to a situation in which feedback on their written work is offered to students.

Viva   In full, viva voce examination, this is when a student is examined in the presence of and in the form of a discussion with two or more academics. For undergraduates (and often Master's students), this would be done to determine a class mark and might be carried out with only selected students, whereas for doctoral researchers it would be the norm, in order to decide on the outcome of a course of study and research.

Weighting   Not all parts of a course or programme are necessarily weighted equally. The third year (or 'part') of a degree programme, for example, might carry twice the credit or 'weight' of the second, whereas the first year might not count towards the final outcome at all. In a similar way, a module outcome might be weighted to favour one piece of assessment over another. The essay might count for two thirds of the overall module mark, while the exam counts for one third, for example. The practice of weighting will vary not only from module to module and between programmes but also between institutions.

RECOMMENDED FURTHER READING

We asked colleagues from a range of universities who run training programmes for teaching in higher education to give their recommendations for further reading. The following are those that they most frequently selected, each with a summary of the comments they made about them.

Biggs, J. and Tang, C. (2007) *Teaching for Quality Learning at University* (3rd edn). Buckingham: SRHE and Open University.

A very detailed book with copious examples to illustrate the theoretical approach adopted and recommended by the authors. It would be useful for more experienced teachers.

Brown, S. and Race, P. (2002) *Lecturing: A practical guide*. Abingdon: Routledge.

A lively and confidence-raising book, helpful for beginning teachers as it shows how to enhance learning through lecturing.

Cowan, J. (2006) *On Becoming an Innovative University Teacher: Reflection in action* (2nd edn). Buckingham: SRHE and Open University Press.

Includes challenging ideas and questions to help develop the practice of all university teachers.

Entwistle, N. (2009) *Teaching for Understanding at University: Deep approaches and distinctive ways of thinking*. Houndmills, Basingstoke: Palgrave Macmillan.

For the teacher with a little experience, a lucid and authoritative overview of research about how teaching can influence learning most productively.

Fry, H., Kettridge, S. and Marshall, S. (eds) (2002) *A Handbook for Teaching and Learning in Higher Education: Enhancing academic practice* (2nd edn). London: Kogan Page.

A practical book, useful as a reference for teachers with a wide range of experience in higher education. It contains case studies, which help ground theory in practice.

Light, G., Cox, R. and Calkins, S. (2009) *Learning and Teaching in Higher Education: The reflective professional* (2nd edn). London: Sage.

Links current thinking about effective learning and teaching to practical experiences within universities.

Race, P (2006) *The Lecturer's Toolkit: A practical guide to learning, teaching and assessment* (3rd edn). Abingdon: Routledge Falmer.

Clearly and accessibly written and very easy to navigate. Particularly useful for beginning teachers with helpful self-assessment questions.

Ramsden, R. (2003) *Learning to Teach in Higher Education*. Abingdon: Routledge Falmer.

Helps readers gain a deeper understanding of educational theories that underpin teaching in the contemporary higher education setting.

You might also like to check Routledge's website for its 'Effective Learning and Teaching in Higher Education' series, which has individual books focusing on different disciplines – modern languages, social policy and social work, engineering, medical, dental and veterinary education, law, mathematics and business and management.

See, too, books by Graham Gibbs, Trevor Habeshaw and Sue Habeshaw, which contain creative ideas for improving teaching in higher education. The following have been updated and are available in print or Kindle format, with others to come in the series:

- *53 Interesting Things to do in your Seminars and Tutorials (Professional and Higher Education)* (5th rev., updated by H. Strawson). Ely: The Professional and Higher Partnership
- *53 Interesting Things to do in your Lectures (Professional and Higher Education)* (5th rev., updated by A. Haynes and K. Haynes). Ely: The Professional and Higher Partnership.

For more information, visit the publisher's website (at: 53interesting. wordpress.com).

We also think that you would find useful information about the higher education teaching context by checking regularly the Quality Assurance Agency's website (at: www.qaa.ac.uk) for information about maintaining quality and standards and current codes of practice, and that of the Higher Education Academy (at: www.heacademy.ac.uk/home), which champions excellence in teaching and learning for a range of services that it offers to the higher education community.

For supportive and illuminating information about a project promoting accessible teaching and learning for disabled students in higher education, visit the Teachability project's website (at: www.teachability.strath.ac.uk).

INDEX